A R L A   S I

Conversations with Insider

Stephen Chua

Foreword by Dr.Michael E. Salla, Ph.D.

The breathtaking revelations of Super Soldier
Stephen Chua, gathered by:

Elena Danaan

ISBN 9798392657988

Illustrations: Elena Danaan

Author's Website: www.elenadanaan.org

Youtube: *"Elena Danaan "*

***

Blessed be the heart of the unsung heroes

In memory of Colonel Stephen Yang Liang Chua

Singapore October 19, 1960 ~ Markham Canada March 6, 2021

***

***

Content

***

Foreword by Dr. Michael Salla

Elena Danaan's communications with Stephen Chua from November 19, 2020, up to his death on March 6, 2021, give the reader an insider's perspective on how highly talented individuals are identified by the military intelligence community of their countries, recruited, and subsequently trained for highly classified projects and special forces. Stephen displayed remarkable psychic abilities as early as three years of age and witnessed gigantic UFOs during his youth in Singapore. His physical skills were also exceptional, and he could successfully hunt wildlife without any formal training to the wonderment of his neighbors. By the time Stephen was 14 years old (1977), he was leading ecotours of the dense Malaysian jungle. He would guide visitors to take photos of wild tigers, elephants, giant snakes, and other exotic species in their natural habitat.

In 1981, Stephen joined the military as part of the Singaporean National Service, which was mandatory for all 18-year-old males. He sat a required IQ test to determine his aptitudes, and his scores were so unbelievably high that he was asked to retake the test three times by incredulous military authorities. The unusual results were reported up the chain of command to senior military officials, and Stephen was identified as among a select group of 12 individuals around the world with such high scores. He was subsequently recruited for Special Forces training and then taken to work directly with the Prime Minister of Singapore—Lee Kwan Yew, who served in that capacity from 1959 to 1990. Stephen spent more than a decade working directly with Lee Kwan Yew, and then from 1990 with his successor Goh Chok Tong who served as Prime Minister up to 2004. Prime Minister Lee was so impressed by Stephen's special abilities and accomplishments as a sniper with Singapore's Special Forces that he was promoted to the rank of Colonel at the age of 21—the first to be awarded such a senior rank at that age.

Elena was able to get a copy of Stephen's military ID, which confirms his military service began in 1981, and she also received a private message from one of Stephen's former colleagues, who confirmed Stephen was in command of an elite military unit. Both documents are reproduced in this book and corroborate key elements in Stephen's testimony.

Stephen describes how he had an extraordinarily high level of gamma wave brain activity, which ranges from 40-80 Hz. Normal humans produce small amounts of gamma waves that govern higher cognitive abilities. His natural ability to produce high levels of gamma waves led to the US military requesting Stephen's transfer to Area 51, where high gamma wave activity was discovered to be critical for successful mind technology interfaces that were being tested on modified jet planes. Prime Minister Lee gave Stephen permission to be reassigned to Area 51 for a short period.

Stephen learned that many US Air Force pilots had suffered severe brain damage or even died when they tried using the mind technology interfaces installed in what he described as an F-15F fighter. These F-15F jets were F-15Es that were specially modified to be flown by thought. He described the special helmet he had to wear and how the co-pilot's back seat was instead filled with electronics. Stephen found that the F-15F had a definite qualitative combat edge over its more conventional F-15E that continues to be widely used today by the US and other national Air Force services. Some kind of serum was used to enhance the pilots' gamma brain activity, but they suffered brain damage, and many died. Area 51 scientists wanted to better understand how gamma waves worked so pilots could use the fly-by-thought planes.

In order to simulate the exacting flying conditions the USAF pilots had to face in piloting the F-15F jets, Stephen was given an accelerated pilots training course at Area 51, presumably the Groom Lake facility, which houses highly classified test aircraft and spy planes. He was able to gain his wings as a test pilot at Area 51 in record time, which is not surprising given the advanced intellectual and physical abilities he had displayed while working with Singapore's special forces.

Stephen succeeded in flying the modified F-15E (F-15F) without touching any instrumentation because his brain could reproduce high levels of gamma waves needed to pilot the plane by thought alone.

Among the scientists working on fly-by-thought projects at Area 51 was a Dr. Jenkins, who worked for the Vatican, according to Stephen. This is where there was an important convergence between Stephen and Elena's testimonies. In the 1980s, when only 16, she was told by one of her extraterrestrial contacts Myrah to find Dr. Jenkins. She later found out that he worked at Wright Patterson Air Force Base, another advanced aerospace testing facility run by the USAF. Apparently, this was the same Dr. Jenkins that Stephen had interacted with at Area 51 around the same time.

Stephen built an antigravity device that could float people and things based on what he had seen at Area 51. The Vatican scientist, Dr. Jenkins, wanted it, so Stephen destroyed the device as he didn't trust the Vatican. Stephen's experience here is similar to an incident involving David Adair, another precocious youngster who gained the attention of USAF officials after he was able to build a small nuclear fusion reactor that was successfully tested at Area 51 in the early 1970s. When Adair realized that his invention was going to be used to build a first-strike nuclear weapon against the Soviet Union, he also decided to destroy it.

While at Area 51, presumably at the more classified S-4 facility at Papoose Lake, Stephen saw Tall Whites (Kiily-Tokurts), as well as a species called the "Maytre," and the ubiquitous short Grays that were worker drones used by many extraterrestrial species including humans. Stephen's testimony corroborates a former US Air Force weatherman, Charles Hall, who says he witnessed Tall Whites at the adjoining Indian Springs facility at Nellis Air Force base in the mid-1960s. Despite being allies, the Tall Whites and Maytre have complex relations that sometimes result in fights. Stephen says the Maytre are particularly aggressive and took an alarmingly keen interest in his abilities. However, they were forced to keep their distance due to the human security guards assigned to protect Stephen from the extraterrestrials.

Stephen describes the spaceport under Area 51 (S-4) and the different ships that used it, including the sinister triangle-shaped ships of the Kiilly Tokurt, again matching what Charles Hall had to say about the Tall Whites ships that regularly flew into underground bases built especially for them. Stephen also described a small shuttle-like space-craft belonging to a fourth extraterrestrial species that were friendly to humans. Apparently, this ship was left alone as the humans were busy trying to replicate the craft belonging to the Tall Whites and Maytre.

Stephen joined a military contingent that boarded a Maytre spacecraft and described a portal system he saw inside the craft that was watery and round. This portal facilitated instantaneous travel to other locations both on Earth and off-planet, which Stephen would later learn to his consternation included his own home. Stephen's description of the portal is very similar to the spacetime portal JP (who currently serves with the US Army) says that he witnessed inside a submerged space ark in the Atlantic Ocean that he visited in February 2022, which I explain at length in my new book, US Army Insider Missions: Space Arks, Underground Cities & ET Contact (2023). JP's experiences with being recruited into the US military and working with Special Forces due to special abilities have important similarities to Stephen's own experiences with elite Special Forces in Singapore.

While at Area 51, Stephen met with Mars-based human technicians who would travel to Earth to work on advanced technologies acquired from different extraterrestrial species. Stephen confirmed that extraterrestrials consider humans to be very good engineers and inventors, and tasked the humans at the bases they jointly occupied to build many advanced technologies. Once again, this aligns with what Charles Hall observed regarding the Tall Whites and their agreements with the US Air Force, which involved the USAF providing many technologies in exchange for advanced aerospace knowledge.

To his great surprise, Stephen learned that the Mars workers temporarily assigned to Area 51 were slaves with few rights. They could be expelled from their Mars bases if they didn't follow orders—a death sentence, given the harsh surface conditions on the red planet.

He described Reptilian extraterrestrials as ultimately in charge of the Mars bases, with other extraterrestrials races, such as the Maytre and short grays being lower in the pecking order.

Stephen's conversations with the Mars-based technicians corroborate other insider reports that an extensive slave trade exists in space that can be traced to the German space program called the Dark Fleet or Nachtwaffen. This is best illustrated in the case of Tony Rodrigues, who describes his harrowing time as a slave while forced to serve on the Moon, Mars, and Ceres during his 20-year abduction, which he describes in his book, Ceres Colony Cavalier: A True Account of One Man's Twenty Year Abduction (2022).

In his communications with Elena, Stephen describes encounters with Reptilian human hybrids sent on assassination attempts, including the then Prime Minister of Pakistan, Benazir Bhutto, during a state visit to Singapore in 1995. Elena provides historical data about Bhutto's visit to Singapore and what Stephen recalled about the incident. What the assassination attempt confirms is that Bhutto had angered the Deep State and it had trained hybrid assassins that would be deployed against designated targets.

In his communications and final interview with Elena, Stephen reveals how his extraordinary talents led to him being harassed and attacked by different extraterrestrial entities for decades, both during and after his service in the Prime Minister's office. During his retirement, Stephen was constantly targeted by those wanting to silence him from ever revealing his experiences. Stephen describes several attacks he received from the Maytre that attempted to eliminate him due to his high gamma brain wave activity that posed a threat to their operations on Earth. Stephen describes how he protected himself throughout his life from attacks, but needed to be rescued once by a Mantid being during one particularly vicious attack by three Maytre who came through a portal—similar to the one Stephen had seen on the Maytre ship while he was at Area 51. The Mantid subsequently healed Stephen of his wounds.

After the decades of attacks took their toll, Stephen realized that his death was not far away, and he decided to contact Elena and reveal to her everything that transpired in his covert missions. His final communications, reprinted in this book, show Stephen's urgency in getting his information out as quickly as possible.

Stephen stated that the sound of Tibetan bowls helps stimulate gamma brain waves and recommends people start listening to them, as well as taking up meditation, and developing love and joy in their lives. Furthermore, Stephen said that as far as technological development is concerned, as long as one develops spiritually through developing gamma brain waves, they will be able to control advanced technologies such as Artificial Intelligence and not be controlled by it. Stephen's advice is similar to how advanced extraterrestrial civilizations such as the Andromedans and Arcturians claim that they are able to safely use Artificial Intelligence due to their consciousness connection to primordial source energy (aka God/Universal Logos, etc.).

Elena Danaan's Area 51: Conversation with Insider Stephen Chua (2023) is a powerful testament to the accomplishments and courage of a brave individual who decided to share his fascinating life story shortly before his death. It is a remarkable book to read and shares many penetrating insights into the secret world of advanced technology projects, Special Forces training, Area 51, and the actions of different extraterrestrial species on Earth. I highly recommend this book as essential reading for those wanting to understand the big picture of what is really happening on Earth.

Michael E. Salla, Ph.D.
May 5, 2023

***

Introduction and Acknowledgments

I wish to express my deepest gratitude to Dr. Michael Salla for his support and guidance, and his initiative to contact me after Stephen Chua passed away. Thanks also to another great supersoldier, Chris O'Connor, for the proof-readings of this book.

I want to acknowledge the courage of Stephen Chua and his resilience in staying alive, waiting for the day when the moment would be right and the world would be ready, so he could tell his story. There are incredible heroes living among us, in anonymity, suffering in silence not to be able to share their intense experience with the public. They signed non-disclosure agreements, received death threats upon themselves and their families, and in the case of Stephen Chua, physical attacks as well. Stephen Chua is a former member of the Singapore Special Forces where he served as a Sniper. In the 1980's at a relatively young age he was also recruited as a Super Soldier. Stephen Chua has repeatedly encountered Reptilian aliens in the Southeast Asia. He served as an experimental pilot in Area 51, working with retro-engineered alien technology. My encounter with Stephen Chua was unexpected. It was a gift from the Universe, as I also believe it was for everyone who got to know him. Except for his enemies, of course. Stephen Chua wasn't a soldier like any other; he was a "bad-ass". Stephen kicked 9Ft tall Reptilian aliens back into their caves, rescued children from monsters, freed villagers from the Khmer Rouge, saved Benazir Bhutto's life, survived an atomic blast, piloted planes with his mind, worked at Area 51, defied Maytra aliens, traveled in a spaceship and met people coming back from Mars.

Stephen was a sniper, body-guard for the Prime minister of Singapore, a pilot in the US Air Force, but he was also a highly spiritual person. This remarkable man trained in martial arts with monks in Tibet, he could levitate, and the most extraordinary of all: Stephen had a very peculiar ability.

His mind could generate Gamma waves up to a level never recorded before. This is the reason why he was taken to Area 51, on a super-secret, highly classified project.

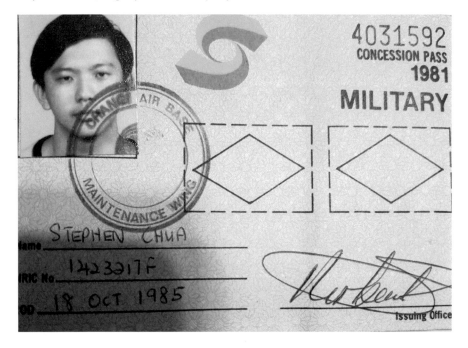

Stephen Chua's military ID

During forty years, Stephen would keep these secrets to himself, enduring regular attacks and threats from the CIA, as well as from extraterrestrial entities. However, whether his body was broken, he kept his determination as strong as steel. Stephen survived only to tell his story... I met Stephen at the occasion of an online interview I gave for Simon Parkes' group Connecting Consciousness Canada, in November 2020. What impressed me first was that Stephen's eyes emanated sweetness and an incredible power at the same time. One could see, through these eyes, a soul that had a tremendous power. Stephen was like a Jedi master inhabiting a broken body. But it wasn't all about his aura and his grounding presence. It was more about something we had in common about which we didn't yet know; our personal links to Area 51, to the same aliens and to one person who worked there in a significant position: Dr. Jenkins.

As we began to communicate via emails and Zoom calls, it turned out that we had matching and complementary info on specific extraterrestrial groups and places. I am sharing in this book all my correspondence with Stephen Chua, the transcripts of our private Zoom calls and of most importance: the transcript of the interview he gave for my YouTube channel and which tragically, four days later, would cost him his life.

It took me a long and painful process to deal with the emotion of Stephen's conditions of departure. It was horrible, it crushed me. How not to feel responsible, in a certain way? Stephen died four days after the public interview he asked me to facilitate for him. He was determined to reveal the truth about Area 51, and nothing, no one, could have stopped him. Nonetheless, I tried to raise his concern about the danger and the potential consequences of going public with his story, but of course, Stephen knew the risks better than anyone else. His health was feeble, his body exhausted with forty years of fighting, and he didn't know how long he had left to deliver the truth.

But still...

I want to express my gratitude to the people from Connecting Consciousness Canada, who put me in contact with Mr. Simon Parkes, the curator of the online event where I met Stephen Chua. His phone call changed my perspective in the aftermath of Stephen's death. Mr. Parkes spoke to me with comforting words, providing me with the missing pieces of the puzzle. He revealed to me that Stephen had first asked him to do an interview about Area 51. Mindful for Stephen's life, same as I had been also, Mr. Parkes warned Stephen against the personal dangers of going public about his experience. But Mr. Parkes said that Stephen was stubborn; he was going to do it anyway because nothing could break his determination. Stephen had also told him that what motivated his sudden decision was in reaction of something that happened: Stephen and "other military personnel" had simultaneously received a death threat from "dark organizations" for speaking out publicly. Why all-of-a-sudden? Were big changes brewing?...

So I learned that Stephen had asked other people before asking me, and he was resolute to speak anyway, in one way or another... These words from Mr. Parkes took the guilt off my mind. He also added:

"Stephen knew the risks, and he chose you, because he knew you were very protected. He chose you to do him the honor of setting him free."

I broke in tears hearing this. The liberating power of words is incredible. So I want to express my gratitude to Mr. Simon Parkes who set me free from this burden by the power of words, as I had myself set Stephen Chua free from forty years of excruciating silence. What a beautiful paying forward. And then, the adventure unfolded onto a new level...

On the following morning, as I was having my breakfast, a blast of energy filled the whole kitchen. Suddenly, in a glorious golden light, appeared a familiar figure, right there in front of me. Stephen; young and ethereal in a magnificent golden armor, was floating above the ground, holding a sword upwards. He looked like in his thirties and in the full embrace of his strength. He said to me:

"I am protecting you as my friend.
Thank you."

Stephen vanished in a haze of shimmering gold, and I remained flabbergasted and paralyzed with awe for a few minutes. I am used to seeing ghosts since my earliest childhood, so my intense emotion wasn't due to fright but to a profound gratitude.

I was sat on my chair, catching my breath, when I heard my phone's notification bell for a new email received. It took me a while to decide to grab my phone, but when I opened my inbox, I smiled with surprise. Dear Stephen, it was you organizing this, wasn't it... I had received my very first email from Dr. Michael Salla, who said he was hoping to connect with me, to talk about Stephen's experience at Area 51. I KNEW this was orchestrated by Stephen! I can't really explain it, but I knew it, deep in my heart.

This email was received precisely at the very moment when Stephen's ghost vanished. I was very impressed that Dr. Salla, a serious and renown figure in the field of Ufology and Exopolitics, contacted me. And a new journey began...

Connecting with Dr. Michael Salla propelled Stephen's testimony into higher levels. I was still processing my emotions and my grief when Dr. Salla interviewed me for the first time.

Massive Intel Dump: Super-Soldiers, Extraterrestrials, Agreements, Interview with Elena Danaan on Death of Stephen Chua (Video)

You can find the transcript of this video, kindly provided by Dr. Salla, at the end of this book. Also, please consult the complete study of this materiel by Dr. Salla on www.exopolitics.org at this link: https://exopolitics.org/supersoldiers-extraterrestrial-agreements-interview-with-elena-danaan-on-death-of-stephen-chua/

The whole world listened. The bird flew out of the cage into the wide, wild world. This was also for me a second phase of liberation. I wish to express my gratitude to Dr. Michael Salla for validating and supporting Stephen Chua's testimony and acknowledging his sacrifice for the disclosure, making it available to a greater number of people.

My heartfelt sympathy goes also to Rebecca Chang, Stephen's wonderful partner, who put her personal life on hold for twenty years, sharing with Stephen his secrets. I contacted her after Stephen's passing and she provided me with corroborations and a scan of his military ID. None of this would have been possible without Rebecca's dedication, resilient support and unconditional love.

***

Meeting Stephen

Here are excerpts of my first contact with Stephen Chua, at the occasion of an interview I gave for Connecting Consciousness Canada on November 19, 2020, about my extraterrestrial encounters. The complete detailed story of my alien abduction at age nine, which is mentioned in this conversation, is available in my book : " A Gift From The Stars"- 2020.

Stephen:
A question for Elena. With your experience with the Grays, did you remember any odors? Smells? Myself I've had one adventure into space with them.

Elena:
Yes, there was. Not on first time because I was too young to remember but yes, actually, I remember smells. The bad ones, they had a smell like ozone or you know, like sulfur.

Stephen:
Yes, it smells more like something coming out of the toilets *(laughs)*. Really, the smell is terrible.

Elena:
Yes it's a kind of smell not enjoyable at all.

Stephen:
Very off-putting. You don't want to get near them.

Elena:
(Mentioning my abductions) One only was smelling like this, the only living entity. The other ones were helpers, they were synthetic life forms. One was a normal living being, and he was smelling, alright! I think he was the supervisor.

Stephen:

Was this the one who is holding a wand?

Elena:

No, it was only helpers but actually, the supervisor passed on the inseminator, a little wand, to a helper, a synthetic one, to put in me. He brought it.

Stephen:

The wand, I asked it is because I spent some time with these life forms. They carry a wand with them, and these are to stun people. It emits a powerful blue light from one end. They point it at your brain and that knocks you out.

Elena:

Ok, no I haven't experienced that. There are so many species as well, you know, who perform abductions, so I suppose they have different techniques.

Stephen:

So these Gray ones, they have a tachyon belt. I haven't experienced with that but yes, they have some nasty stuff. Those are loonies *(laughs)*.

Elena:

Yes these are very frightening. There are many different species. There are the ones from Zeta Reticuli and there are the ones called Solipsirai, that's the small ones. There are as well tall ones, some are called Maytra, it's the tall Grays who are wrinkled and look very hateful.

Stephen:

Angry, yes I remember.

Elena:

These ones are really horrible.

Stephen:

Yes, I was ehm... I was in Area 51.

Elena:

Oh my Gosh, really!

Stephen:

And the people there don't ever look at them in the face. They will try a mental trick on you. They can control you. And if they want something, they don't ask for it, they try to grab it from you.

Elena:

So you met some of them...

Stephen:

Oh yes... too many. They threatened us to kill the army, quite badly, one time.

Elena:

They are very aggressive, aren't they.

Stephen:

Yes, I find them evil, really.

Elena:

Yes, you think evil inhabits them, that there's no hope, that they are pure emanation of evil. That's how they look like. And the feel of them, isn't it.

Stephen:

Yes, they have their aura. You just feel it: "keep your distance" *(laugh)*.

Elena:

That's very interesting that you worked there.

Stephen:

I was part of the Air Force. They were developing flight-by-thought systems. Flying and weaponry. So the trouble is, that system requires a lot of Gamma waves from the brain. Very strong, very definite gamma waves. And they use artificial means; unfortunately, the pilots won't last very long, the brain just turns to mash. They asked me because I had very natural Gamma. I guess this was alien technologies. Backwards engineered fighter planes, F-15 F or F-15 Eagle. The rear pilot seat was covered with electronics. So when you are flying, they put that helmet on you with things sticking out of it. That was to measure the brainwaves. What we found was that simulated flights are never near as fast and efficient, so I had to do the electral flights, electron meta sequences and such. And they found that, that was truly over a hundred time faster than any computer. So these planes are incredible. I was a very young man, I was sent there by my prime minister and you know, *(laughs)* you've got to do it!

Commentaries:

I documented the extraterrestrial species Stephen referred to, the Maytra, in my book "A Gift From The Stars" published in August 2020. Here is an excerpt of the relevant section :

Maytra *(pl. Matrei)*, or Maitre, originate from two home planets in the nearest galaxy of Andromeda, that they name Megopei. They are your worst enemy, and the worst enemy of all races in this galaxy. They are considered as parasites by everyone except by those who managed to create alliances of mutual interests with them: the Ciakahrr Empire and the Orion collectives. Of the same average height as humans, this race of hermaphrodites with long shaped face, elongated skull and long slim neck, carries a very mean look. Their motivations are rage, hate and assimilation. Their ships are large, dark and discoidal with a circular row of lights plus a large aperture underneath, and their insignia is a black inverted triangle on 3 lines and a red background.

Maytra tall Gray from the Andromeda galaxy, similar to those encountered by Stephen Chua in Area 51

***

Email correspondence

Email, November 25 2020/ Elena Danaan to Stephen Chua

Hi Stephen,

I was compelled to contact you, since this Zoom group video. Your testimony about the tall Gray beings resonated with me, and I wished to exchange the info we both have, to try to understand. I would personally like to know what happened to you, when you were working there in Area 51. I would love to hear your story, and help you in the measure of my capabilities.

The beings I was told about by my ET contacts, that are in relation with Area 51, are of two kinds: the first type of extraterrestrials are named the Maytra (or Maitre), these are pure evil and hateful inter-dimensional entities. Please find joined to this email some drawings and info, and you can tell me if they were the same ones that you had to deal with. The other type is the Kiily-Tokurt, or Tall Whites.

I was also selected by the CNRS (National Center for Scientific Research) in France, to enroll as a guinea pig for remote-viewing and psychic spying experiments, in coordination with the French National Space Agency, but I escaped and moved to Ireland. This I do no tell people, but I feel we both have secrets that have marked our lives. I do not tell everything in my book, for reasons you may understand yourself. *(note: I since published this anecdote in my book "The Seeders"-2022)*

I also have info about piloting alien ships. I have been shown a few things and explained how some ships are made and how they work. Piloting by mind, I have seen them doing that. I also can see fairies and ghosts since I was born, and of course aliens. It is sometimes hard to live in a world full of predators when we see more than we should. I would love to know your story in Area 51.

I hope my documents will make sense to you.

Kindest regards,

Elena

Email, November 26 2020 / Stephen Chua to Elena Danaan

Dear Elena,

So good to hear from you. I have been having this feeling you had sent me a message. You are very intriguing. Somehow, I feel I know you from a long time ago. I do not normally talk about those things and events.

And I feel also that you can feel something is not right with me. Yes, it's the Maytra who has been attacking me. Recently I was under the influence of a possession and I was severely tortured with one severe affliction after another. In fact, I am still recovering from the last episode. I have since detached it from me with the help of a close friend.... love is the key. It was a most painful experience.... emotionally and physically. But the price was we were almost killed in an auto-crash; we were transporting the beast who had used an item as a portal, away to be dumped, but inside the car suddenly went foggy and we crashed severely. Amazingly, we were not injured. However, I was attacked one last time as the next day my legs and arms had turned completely coal black. Then I saw the beast sitting on my bed which almost freaked me out.

Now I understand what people suffering from possessions by an evil is like. As a child I was sometimes brought to a possessed person; usually another child and I merely played with them and the evil left immediately. I can see the evil being, and tell it to leave because I don't like it and it does. And so it goes even until recently. However, the possession attack has also damaged my energy and my memories of healing simply is now gone.

Once upon a time, I was trained and developed in the use of energy, as a fighting force and to heal. Injuries such as gunshot wound[s] or broken bones can be healed overnight. I was also trained as a Chinese medicine doctor by the age of 22. The ones who trained me lived in an isolated part of Tibet and live hundreds of years (a 2 hundred year old man may only look like 45 yrs. or so). There, they had contact with 8.5 ft. tall people who live underground.

Yes, I once had great strength and ability, but a nuclear blast took most of it away. I was in the military and on mission to rescue over 2,000 very young children. At the time, I already had the ability to fight with swords although I was never taught. Apologies for being long winded but it's just a gist of being me.

In Area 51 I was sent there because all that development created a being who used Gamma waves far more than Alpha in my brain. I could even project Gamma waves several meters from my body. Also, being a highly accomplished military man, I was the Prime Minister's bodyguard, nominated with the authority of a Field Marshal, the world's youngest Colonel in rank, best sniper (won numerous world war games), I was also a pilot, I've had many missions into enemy territory and accomplishing objectives. My main mission was to keep the Khmer Rouge from attacking Thailand. Hence I was selected among many candidates for Area 51. They needed a natural Gamma wave person because their own pilots who had artificial Gamma enhancements die from brain lesions.

There were tall and small Grays there. And yes, the Maytra also made an occasional appearance but always under strict armed security. I could feel their energy which was truly like an angry animal...like a tiger. I was first trained to fly an F15 -f (Eagle) fighter.

Then it was a solo flight with the necessary electronics in the co-pilot seat. Here, I flew the plane without holding the controls. The firing was also done by thought. After a few days, I found I could fly and do many operations without even physically activating anything with a response time over a hundred times faster than physical operations.

So in the several war games we operated in, they found nothing to compare. I won the exercises even with 6 planes to 1. Fly by thought is amazingly effective but the Air Force canceled its development. I was invited into a Gray space ship to transport me to another location. However, as I observed their operation on the various panels, I was told to stop transmitting (my brain waves) as it interfered with the on board flight systems.

Many things happened which ended up with me running from Singapore. I was given the green light to Canada within a few hours of my application, and it was a lifetime of life and death cat and mouse games with assassins. It's a same, a whole brigade of promising young men and women were injured beyond recovery (I do not kill but will damage attackers severely).

Fast forward till a few years ago. I was wondering why there were dark shadows and small imps bothering me. And yes, by now my body had been suffering for many years in extreme pain, and no way to heal myself as that ability had been remove from me by that nuclear blast. A tall black being attacked me from behind. My back kick sent it into a brick wall which left an imprint. The fighter in me still put up a fight but where my foot made contact with it was a burning sensation. During the next full moon I awoke in great pain as I saw and felt as though something was trying to rip my soul from my body. At the same time my heart felt like its energy was being depleted. 'I fought back hanging on and then I could see a portal into another world with 3 beings with arms raised and trying to draw my energy through. Then a huge energy wave came blasting from behind me with such force it blew the 3 beings off their feet. I collapsed and awoke in a strangely clean place. There were a couple of very tall

beings giving me some kind treatment and easing my chest and soul energy centers. I felt no fear but felt comforted. I asked to see and remember them. One appeared to me while gently holding my hand. It was a doctor, a Mantid. He gave a message but I do not remember it and fell asleep.

Your memory is excellent, with your pictures. I wish to be able to tap into the energy of knowledge again. Since the possession attack, I suffered at least 2 strokes which really terminated that ability which is replaced by fear and phobias. I am recovering but I know I need far more help there. I can't yet seem to heal myself. I've lost my Gamma wave ability.

Thank you for reminding me with those pictures. It may be the start of remembering me. As for fairies, I sometimes walk in forests just to say hello to them. And ghosts? Well I stay away from hospitals. Many ghosts are actually remote-viewing beings and sometimes Djinns. Normally I would not be so bold as to ask for help but I feel you have knowledge which can put me on that path. Thank you...love...

Stephen Chua

Email, November 26, 2020 / Elena Danaan to Stephen Chua

Dear Stephen,

Last night after I read your email, I had intense dreams of being in the cockpit of a narrow plane (Earth made, not ET), with strange commands. There was a screen in front of me with weird holographic patterns moving very fast. The plane was going so fast, above and through the clouds. I could hear the sound of the engine, that is how I know it was Earth made. Was I connecting to some memories of yours? I had this impression.

The resume of your life at service is mind-blowing and your accounts of Area 51 with the Maytra matches so well, too well, my experience with them. Especially when you mentioned the animal aggressiveness emanating from them, as a "tiger energy"... it is exactly the feel I get from them! Tiger-like energy! I was confronted to one of them by my contact, Thor Han, the Nordic alien who rescued me: they caught a Maytra as a prisoner, on their ship, and Thor Han connected to me by telepathy to show me this being held behind a containment energy field.

27

It was like the vision of the worst nightmare... the Maytra was hysterical, like a tiger caught in a cage. Very frightening stuff, and the hate and evilness from him, oh my gosh... This is the drawing I sent you in my last email. Have you seen yourself this symbol of theirs (the Maytra): the black triangle crossed by 3 lines? I suppose they were residing in the lower underground levels at Groom Lake, working with US army personnel on despicable projects, am I correct? I know there are also other Gray races there, such as the Kiily-Tokurt for instance (Tall Whites).

I was also shown the inside of a "Nordics" ship, and how to pilot it. They let me sit in a pilot seat, twice, and showed to me they different options regarding if you travel short planetary distance or subspace long distance. There was a way for thought-piloting, linking the mind of the pilot to the "mind" of the ship, using an implant in their head. Certain species don't need an implant. They sit in the chair, first they set a target on a monitor and then they put their hands on hexagonal patches on the sides of the chair, and this connects their mind to the ship's navigation by their DNA. You must know better than me about these things, I am sure. To what race belonged the Gray ship you were on, for this short ride you describe?

When I was a teenager, a Nordic alien lady appeared in my bedroom and transformed my wall into a screen, throughout which I could see ships (flying saucer-like) landing in a desert, and then a flight by night (as if I was in the ship), over a complex of buildings in a desert area. She was pointing out to me a special hangar and repeated these words: "you must contact Dr Jenkins". What could a frightened teenager dare be doing with that info? Nothing, of course. I was too scared. It turned out that recently, I checked out on Google to see if this vision corresponded to some place and I was shocked to discover it matched perfectly an aerial view of Area 51. Would you by any chance know of a Dr Jenkins who would have worked there? My contact with this alien lady was in the early eighties. Although, I found by a Google search, a certain Dr. Jenkins who worked in the cognitive department at Wright-Patterson. These two places are linked, as you and I know.

Regarding possession... The secret, from my experience, is to cast fear out of your world. Indifference and compassion are our best weapons. This is how they get us and hold power upon us: fear. You need to rebuild yourself, rebuild your confidence in your own power, reclaim your being, your body, your soul, your sovereignty.

You have been damaged, not destroyed. You are still alive, and as long as you are alive you can fight. I have this insight that you need to emit Gamma waves again. You were trained, you know how to do that. Sound can help you. There are tuning forks that create a Gamma binaural sound, you stick both on either side of your head and they traverse your skull and brain with Gamma waves.

You need to reactivate, in order to take back your power. The entities of the shadow wanted to get rid of you, you know why? Because you are more powerful than them. They are the ones who fear you. They tried to reverse the situation but in truth, they are the ones who fear. Because you can see them, and because you can destroy them.

If they ever approach you again, stand up to them and claim that you don't fear them, and by the power of your own will, cast them away. Mentally, energetically, and physically. You could do such thing before, and you will again. I know this! I would like to offer you my book, because it may help you as it has helped already so many people. If you feel unsafe to give me your address, you can give me the address of a friend I can send it to. Otherwise, I have the PDF (but the paperback is nice to have, it is up to you, you tell).

Ok that was a long email, but there is so much to say. With time. Light be around you, and within you.

Elena

Email, November 27 2020 / Stephen Chua to Elena Danaan

Dear Elena,

Sounds like you connected with a moment of my experience. That was during a dog-fight sequence; yes, very intense focus. It was particularly powerful because of the mental energy I had to use to operate all the systems simultaneously, which is why non-Gamma humans cannot fly such a machine and the project was abandoned some years later.

Actually, militarily, my team and I had battled a team of Ciakahrrs in an isolated part of Malaysia. There was nothing glorious about it, as we barely got away with our lives. They moved so fast and countered everything we did. They also had energy weapons which simply outgunned our team of crack snipers. I carried uranium explosive rounds which helped slow their advance. I was also carrying a new weapon called a neutron grenade which is a small nuclear explosive launched by bazooka. I fired one into the giant mountain cavern they were in, and the blast collapsed the entire mountain. We ran for our dear lives.

I've also encountered and battled hybrids of human n Ciakahrr (captured a few of them).

I was approached by a Dr. Jenkins while in the military (early eighties) because they found I had created a new form of energy device and also a new type of light-weight structure with ordinary materials. He appeared to be working for the Vatican and I did not trust the whole organization.

The Grey ship I was in was piloted by small Grays; one natural, the other 4 were androids, but the one in charge was a tall one. There were 4 humans seated in a corner of the ship as passengers. The seats being rudimentary but secure. Your drawings of that ship brings memories of a different time.

I know my brain Gamma needs to be reactivated, however I feel I need a trigger to bring it back spontaneously. I keep getting flashes of events from lives of a long time ago. So, who am I? Why am I the way I am.? What did I do of such significance??? I've been meditating and receiving spontaneous dreams. Also, during waking hours, I am experiencing missing time. For example, I was staring at an ant beside my foot and then as I looked up my clock told me 2 hours had passed. Will regressive hypnosis help I wonder? Maybe if I knew my star family too might help...

I'd love to have your book if I can afford it as I am on government disability.

Many thanks, Love and light.

Stephen Chua

November 27 2020 /Stephen Chua to Elena Danaan

Dear Elena,

I meant ask you this question...Do you know much about Auric Fields? I used to see Auric Fields. My Auric Field is very weakened recently.

During and after the possession, there was a dark field enveloping me directly, draining my energy. I saw this and with help from a friend we had pushed it some distance from my body. It is no longer in direct contact with my body but still all around me. It seems to block my reception to the source and feeds really bad vibes and memories. Do you have any ideas to break this dark energy?

Thank you. Love.

Stephen Chua

Email, November 29 2020 / Elena Danaan to Stephen Chua

Hello Stephen,

I was first flabbergasted to read you were approached by a Dr Jenkins... this is so mind-blowing to me... Myrah, the alien lady who appeared in my bedroom to show me this aerial view of Area 51, was telling me at the time that I needed to find him. I never knew the reason why. I know this man held answers to many questions but now, as time passed, I do not feel I want to contact him. It is like a past story. Although, your words come like a splash of consciousness to me: an old memory being suddenly "real stuff", "real name", "real people".

Quite amazing that I was connected to one of your memories of a flight-sequence. As if it was showing me that I could connect to your consciousness, because maybe I can help you.

The Ciakahrrs... They are in my book (which I will send you this Monday by post). And all you write about them matches with what Thor Han (my contact) told me. When Thor Han was transmitting to me by telepathy the info for the book, came the chapter about the Ciakahrrs and it was so upsetting, so shocking, that I stood up to go and throw up in the bathroom. This is horrendous what is going on underneath our ground... Nightmares are a pale echo of what is happening. You know, no need for me to go further on this topic. Yes, they make hybrids to create an enhanced combat elite. Impressive that you captured a few of them, I would listen to your stories for hours... because it matches all I have been told. I really feel for you, having dealt with that. I can't wait to hear your feedback about my book and hear your stories, because I am sure it will reactivate parts of your memory, and give you keys, as it has done already for many people.

I do believe you need first to reactivate your Gamma brain, and there is a tremendous healing to do first. Regressive hypnosis is a good tool but not yet, not in the state you are in at the moment; you need to be strong again first, emotionally, because regressive hypnosis brings up memories and emotions you need to be ready to deal with.

You need to stay protected and as discrete as possible. I have told no one at all that I am communicating with you by email. You are a target at the moment for those who fear that you awaken, and also because you were involved in Area 51 and secret projects. I would be very careful to who you speak to. There are ears everywhere. If they know you are back up and running, they may try to get in the way but... it is to their own loss, because when you wake up, you can destroy them. I am speaking about the Maytra & friends. They are the ones who fear, not you. They use fear against you to make you believe you are weak and vulnerable, but in truth, this is a trick.

But heal first, get back on your feet, and then you can face the past. I wanted to offer you a present also, the reason is I know exactly the right item. So you will receive by UPS a set of binaural brain tuner forks. I have the same ones and they are so powerful. When you receive them, please contact me and via Zoom, I will show you how to use them and we can work together. Also, I want to show you protections I know. That would be great anyway to chat via Zoom.

As I was saying to you in the last email, you have been damaged, not destroyed. I see auric fields too. Sit and enter a meditative state. Visualize at your plexus chakra, a ball of bright energy, growing and pulsing, a golden-white energy. Spin it faster and faster, and extend it outwards, slowly but surely, and it is going to cleanse your auric field as it grows, and push back darkness. If you lose it, focus again on your chakra to create a second one, and expand it again. please do this every morning. It doesn't take a lot of time but it is going to start to cleanse your energy field. All is about visualization. I have a YouTube channel where I put free videos about how to protect yourself, and meditations.

With love, light and joy.

Elena

Dear Elena,

Thank you so much for the vote of confidence and tip. Yes, I found that with the third chakra expansion, color and spin, it felt like the sun. I had forgotten the power of sunlight within. This act pushes and disperses the dark cloud around me but a little later the dark cloud reforms a little at a time. Although it does not touch me it still interferes with my connection to source knowledge. It sends dark messages to me, however I found I remember in flashes of what that dark energy being was doing to me. I can break through its shielding or lies...

I really am surprised by your ability to connect to my energy... perhaps a higher power is acting on our behalf?

Shielding protection is what I used throughout my life. It saw me through my military missions. The invisibility is especially effective. You see, as a child, I used to hunt for my food. And yes, childhood was a trying and dangerous time of my life too. I'm still surprised I survived it. At 3years of age I was thrown down a cliff but a being restored my broken body; witnessed by my Grandmother. And again, a few months later, I was poisoned and as I was dying and almost dead, that same being woke me up and took me by the hand. We flew over the rooftops and I could see a very long distance over many farms. There were 2 white doves on the roof of our home and I could see my grandparents arriving in a car. I was brought back into my body and I sat up in front of my Grandmother. The being's name is (the Chinese call her this) Kwan Yin.

The attempts to kill me was because of money....lots of it. Oh, a little secret, I could levitate as a child and in my martial arts training that same energy was used to good effect. Yes, please let me know when we can further the treatment online....I am ready.

Stephen Chua

Email, December 2 2020 / Elena Danaan to Stephen Chua

Dear Stephen,

You are starting to remember your power, that it is there, it was always there, and they just threw smoke in your eyes, and pain in your body, to convince you that your power was gone. But it never was...

I believe, as I think I start to understand it, that benevolent higher powers as you say (maybeQwan Yin), put me on your path to help you gain your confidence and power back. I am available next Wednesday (Dec 9) after 11pm UTC. Hopefully in the meantime you will have received the tuning forks and we can work together with this too. Now is the time you reclaim your power xxx

Elena

ZOOM CONVERSATION DECEMBER 9 2020

I was just setting up my computer, getting ready to click on the Zoom link to open my communication with Stephen, when a glass of water fell on it without me touching it. I switched my laptop off and swiftly turned it upside down on a towel. In panic, I grabbed my phone and managed to send Stephen a new link, which worked using the phone. As it would turn out later, my laptop died. Fortunately, all the data could be retrieved. Stephen sensed a Maytre near him, so we raised stronger energy protections. Stephen eventually felt the intruder going away. I didn't understand why my laptop was attacked, because my guides and protectors had shielded me with protection previously to this communication. Stephen guessed that the attack happened at the very moment I clicked on the Zoom link, when it linked me to his malevolent watchers.

We worked together on the use of the binaural Gamma tuning forks, trying to reconnect the damaged pathways in his brain.

Stephen:

They attack me a lot. I had two strokes this year, but the possession was the most frightening. I've never been so frightened before in my life. Because you know, I never know when I'm going to be attacked again. Each time, it leaves a massive infection on me, arms and legs all at once, overnight.

And there's this thing that happened, it's so frightening. I decided to reach out to Simon Parkes, but as I started to type my letter, I was suddenly attacked by a wave of energy. It froze the keyboard and my body was instantly covered by rashes, even my face. As stubborn as hell, I kept going. Next thing, my legs were hurting like crazy and when I looked down, there were holes near my ankles. I still kept going, but you see how vicious this thing is. On the following morning, my feet were covered by red hexagonal patches. I pulled one and it had a moving tail that was stuck into my flesh, sucking my blood. I have had a lot of attacks, this is just a small part. They try to scare me, and hurt me every time I try to seek speak to someone.

In this other place I was living in, someday I had this feeling somebody was trying to pull my heart out, or my soul out. It felt pulled out and when I looked up, there was this portal that opened, a large one, and there were three of them there. They were drawing the energy from me. I fought them of course. Suddenly, there was this huge mass of energy coming through, from behind me, and it blasted them. The portal shut. So there was somebody that protected me, then. I felt falling down back on the bed and I said to myself: "I want to remember!". Next thing, I am looking up at this Mantid. He was healing my chest. He was very friendly, a very kindly type of Mantid. He had these very long fingers that touched me. He told me that they were trying to steal my soul.

36

Stephen:

One time in my military career, I was hit by an atomic bomb. Eighty five soldiers died. I was alive. I was blown into the water, but the blast was enough to take away all my abilities. I had fantastic psychic or energy abilities, whatever they want to call it, and I was able to use energy to knock people down, levitate, and whatever it is, it was gone, it was taken away from me. But there was something that shielded me from death, because the blast was incredible. Everything around was black.

You know, I have seen some spaceships, people who took off in these Grays' spaceships, I've seen a lot of those. But this one, I never knew who it belonged to. It was pill-shaped one, long, about 50 Ft across, and about 8 Ft in diameter. I've seen some of them pretty close up. These ones are white, very glowing white. I've seen them cleaning the atmosphere from chem-trails, as well. Which is quite an amazing watch. I've seen a ship that's about 2km long, very close to ground. It was during a very heavy storm, full of clouds everywhere. You could see this cloud going 90 degrees against the wind. It was kind of weird. I told my captain and he said : "no this is a ship coming by." It was supposed to be, I think, shielded. It was elongated shape, with some structures outside sticking out of it. It had a round cross-section, but it was elongated like a cigar.

In Area 51, I was given access to parts of an aircraft that was put in the storage. I took them out and I played with one. So immediately, it started to levitate. You can put these batteries, each battery is like 80 kg each, heavy. You put a battery on that contraption and it won't budge, it keeps floating. And of course, some people hear about it, and it's when this Dr. Jenkins came around. And I figured from what he told me that he worked with the Vatican.

US Navy aircraft carrier Nimitz was terrorised by a squadron of brilliant white, super-agile aircraft resembling tic tac candy, similar to the description made by Strephen Chua.

Stephen:

And when you have the knowledge of the Vatican, what they do, the inventions, and to people, it's very bad! So I don't trust them. So what I did was I ripped it all off, the contraption, and he asked to put it back together and I said "no". They wanted it! I'm not giving it to you (laughs)! This Dr. Jenkins, he was a paramilitary, but dark still. I am a bit psychic and I could tell he was lying to me, and when he mentioned the Vatican, I asked a couple of questions on the Vatican. That is where his loyalty was, the Vatican.

Elena:

I was asked by this "Nordic" alien woman to contact Dr. Jenkins, because he knew, he would bring all the answers. She knew that this man knew a lot of things.

Stephen:

It think maybe it was the time when he hadn't turned his loyalty to the dark side yet, and maybe talking to you he would have seen something.

Elena:

You know I was fourteen years old and I was like: no way, that is frightening me! I just blanked everything. I'm totally mind-blown that she showed me Area 51 by flight, by consciousness flying above it, and she told me the name of this man! It was absolutely mind-blowing. And she was showing me a hangar, a particular rectangular hangar. There was something in there, and this hangar was on the side of a slope, a little rocky hill. There was like a road, crossing over, and it was on the left, and... there were series of hangars, and this one was...

Stephen:

Did it back up to a mountain?

Elena:

Yeah.

Stephen:

OK it's only a small part of the building, because the rest of it is under the mountain.

Elena:

Ok, so it was the entrance of an underground facility, that's why she was showing it to me. Why she was showing this to me as a young person, I don't know. I was in France, I was fourteen, there wasn't anything I could do. She was insisting on this place, that this place was holding answers.

Stephen:

Maybe you could access it by remote-viewing.

Elena:

I'm not sure, it may be kind of protected against remote-viewing.

Stephen:

Oh yeah they will watch you. Outside, the security is very tight, I mean, but inside it's very casual. I've had two guides. When I was moving from place to place. Their job was keeping the aliens away from me. They didn't carry normal guns, they had these energy weapons. The bullets don't work on these guys.

Elena:

It was the Maytre, that you saw there, isn't it?

Stephen:

Yes, but the Maytra wasn't common. They do appear once in a while. The most you see is little Grays, all over the place. You wonder why they're so rude all the time, it's because they're androids.

Commentaries:

What follows are excerpts from my 2020 book "A Gift From The Stars", when my friend Myrah physically beamed up into my bedroom. Myrah is a "Nordic" alien lady from the Sirius B star system, who was part of the crew who rescued me from Gray aliens at age 9:

"My next memory leaps to April 1983 in Marseille, when I was thirteen years old. I woke up one night sat on my bed, facing the wall, sweating and breathless, my heart beating very fast. I saw something that looked like a screen in the wall with images of a weird landscape, with a hill towards which people were running in haste, and red glowing spaceships coming down from the sky to rescue them. Then, this beautiful alien woman appeared very vividly in the wall in front of me. She had soft pale skin, big wide green eyes, rosy lips, her hair was blond and straight, and she looked very serious. She was wearing a skin-tight shimmering blue uniform and a golden metallic belt with tiny devices attached to it. She said to me:

"Find Doctor Jenkins in Ohio!"

Then suddenly, behind her, I saw like if I was flying above a deserted landscape with a series of buildings (in my later research it turned out it was area 51, which is not in Ohio but wait for what follows...). The voice of the alien woman was repeating: "Find Dr Jenkins!".

Then, her face showed up again with a very imperative expression and she immediately disappeared like switching off a TV monitor. I did some research about this vision recently, and in Ohio there is a military facility well known for being involved with aliens and UFOs: Wright-Patterson USAF, in Dayton. And you will never guess: not only is the Ohio military base related to the Roswell crash and area 51, but a Doctor Jenkins worked there at the time I was thirteen. I never dared or had the courage to try to contact him, even though he surely possessed some key information for me. Why me? Why him? "

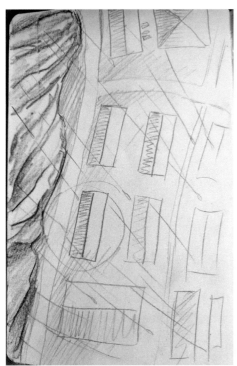 

Comparison between a drawing by Elena Danaan made in 1983 (left), and an aerial view of Area 51. Identical buildings can be identified.

Myrah beaming up in my room and transforming my wall into a holographic screen.

Email, December 12 2020 /Stephen Chua to Elena Danaan
(After the zoom video call)

Dear Elena,

You and Thor Han's message brings me some peace... my appreciation. Remembering one of the Maytre encounters - they have a device which seems to emit lightning to attack, shock and burn their victims. I also noticed they carry fungal parasites on their bodies. I had an urge, perhaps a message to put the great blue star within me... Connect this blue star energy with my soul. It does feel warm and I feel greater energy to move around. Loving all you're doing for humanity....

Commentary:

After two months without any news from Stephen, I began to worry. What if something had happened to him? He renewed contact on a different tone. He was in a hurry, I could feel an energy of stress and urge coming from his messages. They were short, sharp, and to the point. No time for conversation, just a desperate call for help.

Email, February 24 2020 /Stephen Chua to Elena Danaan

Dear Elena,
I know you've been busy.
Would you have any scheduling for an interview?
I'm ready to speak.

Stephen Chua

Email, February 24 2020 / Elena Danaan to Stephen Chua

Hi Stephen,

Are you sure...? I was thinking this Friday 26th at 6pm EST? (11pm UTC here in Ireland). We will record it first, and I will edit it and put it on YouTube after.

Are you really sure you want to do this?

Elena

Email, February 25 2020 /Stephen Chua to Elena Danaan

OK Friday 6. 00pm EST sounds good. I'm scheduled.
Thank you.

Stephen Chua

Commentary:

The interview was recorded via Zoom, on Friday February 26. I could feel we had a lot of protections. I promised Stephen to edit it for covering his face and do something nice, and that I will air it on the following Sunday, March 7, 2020. On the following day, Stephen got back to me with his feedback and impressions from our recording:

Email, February 24 2020 /Stephen Chua to Elena Danaan

Dear Elena,

The interview was so effective I've more memories of events coming back.

- before being possessed, I was being attacked first by a tall thin shadow being. It came up from behind me at home. I could sense it and lashed out with a kick. I could feel hard contact with it and a terrible burning pain on my heel. However, that being was sent flying into the wall where it left a dark imprint with a hard impact.

- over the next several months I was being observed by people in black helicopters.

- A few weeks later, I woke up one night with some energy dragging me from my chest and torso. I could see and feel my soul being drawn out. Of course I resisted regardless of pain and shock. And I could see a portal and on the other side were three Maytre (they wore a bluish type of cloak and gown with that typical triangle symbol with three stripes) working some kind of energy spell on me. It felt like a losing battle until I saw a massive wave of swirling energy blast through that portal from behind me sending the three tumbling and the portal was shut. I then collapsed.

- I awoke with a very large Being removing some probes from my chest and head. And I could hear telepathically him telling me that He is just making sure the damage to my heart was corrected.

Your soul is strong he told me. It was then I could see the Being. He had no hands like ours but long elegant fingers that are so gentle. I somehow knew that he was a Mantid, known to be excellent doctors. We actually chatted. He wanted to make sure I wasn't brain damaged. I called him Dr. Trixy (his language had a lot of clicks and the human tongue cannot pronounce their words) and he was pleased. I fell asleep....

- I observed other E.T.s clean up the chem-trails in the sky. This was a white pill shaped ship about 15 meters long. It was also outside my window for a few minutes. From another location, I saw, during a massive storm, a ship at least 2 kilometers long (it was ovoid in shape) flying at right angle to the clouds, right overhead of my bedroom window.

-During military days, I had encountered another kind of E.T. ...These were like the gargoyles and had wings. There were three of them which confronted me and my team. They have mind control ability. I ordered my team not to look at them as I faced them (they couldn't control me).

-When I was a teen, I would regularly encounter crypto creatures, but I wonder if they were actually E.T. Remember I said I used a stick to fight? Well I used that stick and battled a number of them, usually in the middle of the night. They came to steal animals from our farm. They had claws and one even had a weapon like a sickle.

I can sense there were encounters with the Maytre which I can't quite remember yet...wish I can.

I'll send you more as I recall them.

Thank you...

Stephen Chua

The confrontation with winged gargoyle-like ET's fit the description of Alpha Draconis Ciakahrr extraterrestrials.
(Illustration from "A Gift From The Stars"-2020)

Email, February 27 2020 / Elena Danaan to Stephen Chua

Hi,
I am editing the video and I would like to know, the boss of Area 51 is the United States Space Force, isn't it? Is that what you said? With this logo?

Elena

Email, February 27 2020 /Stephen Chua to Elena Danaan

This logo is the current space force. The old one was different...it did not have the sphere inside the circle.

Stephen Chua

Email, February 27 2020 / Elena Danaan to Stephen Chua

Thank you! I want to insert the logo in the video for a few seconds when you talk about it. Would you be able, when you have time, to find the right one please? That would be awesome :)
Thank you!

Email, February 27 2020 /Stephen Chua to Elena Danaan

This was the one the human general was wearing.

Stephen Chua

Email, February 27 2020 / Elena Danaan to Stephen Chua

Hi!

Here is the link for you to download a copy of the edited video. Tell me what you think if you are ok for me to post it, or if you want to modify stuff. I will post it next Sunday, then if you have other memories coming in the meantime, I will add them as I did, as a little inserted text.

Please still consider if you think it is safe for you enough to do this.

Elena

Email, February 28 2020 /Stephen Chua to Elena Danaan

Wow, you turned it into a movie. I like it, although if you have time, perhaps reduce the written fonts little? And extend it's time.
Thanks....
Wow! I like it. Please put it up.

THANK YOU!

Stephen Chua

Email, March 1 2020 /Stephen Chua to Elena Danaan

Dear Elena,

I know I'm toughing it out but I'm still blacking out, something severely oppressive ...may not make the week. But here's more...

In 1982 there was this massive drought in Africa and the Somalian people were dying of starvation. The UN was simply arguing about how much medicine to send them...those idiots forget that people live on food, not drugs. In the end, they used the US military to drop via parachutes tons of wheat. They also do not understand these people do not eat wheat. But in South East Asia was a bumper crop of everything. Farmers were throwing away rice, tapioca, vegetables, fish and what else. So food was cheap. I organized with my bosses, 2 freight ships and filled them with preserved salted fish, salted vegetables, tapioca flour, sweet potato, rice, salted mutton, and several other foodstuffs. We sent them ships to Somalia but to our dismay there was already a ship sunk on dockside. I was asked to come and solve the issue. Well, since there were tens of thousands of people on dock, we used gang-plancks; several goes across the sunk vessel and then onto our ship, one by one. Thus within a week all our food was dispatched and distributed. I heard that it fed the starving population for almost a month. When news got around the world, grass roots organizations collected food to send. This was the beginning of a movement called Food Aid.

In 1983 there was this massive storm , a hurricane hitting Bangladesh.about 10 million people were without food. Again the UN hawed and hummed and talked about medicines. Well, South East Asia still had another bumber crop. This time I ordered 5 freighters and sent them on. there was no dock to use but the Indian government were glad to have the food and send them on. They couldn't help with food supplies simply because the storm had destroyed their crops too. But sending rice, tapioca flour, salted vegetables, salted meats, salted fish was what was needed to prevent starvation. Again, Food Aid took hold and many organizations made sure they got enough food.

Remember this term....FOOD AID.

Stephen Chua

Email, March 1 2020 /Stephen Chua to Elena Danaan

Several months ago, after I had thrown off the evil bunny, as I slept, a team of human (I saw their eyes) came through a portal in my bedroom and tried to suppress me. One had his knee on the back of my neck and the other was trying to extract something from my arm.

Well, they had a surprise as I managed a few kicks of my own and knocked both of them down. I wasn't in good health otherwise they wouldn't be getting up. As it was, they crawled into their portal. Never seen them since. But they had injured me at the back of my neck and there was a nasty cut on my arm.

Anyway, right now, after watching the interview, I am feeling really a very heavy weight on my chest and I'm blacking out through heart congestion and shortness of breath. Something's attacking me....

Once again, Thank you.

Stephen Chua

Email, March 3 2020 /Stephen Chua to Elena Danaan

Dear Elena,
I'm suffering blackouts and I'm throwing up blood.
so, the sooner the story comes out the better.
Stephen Chua

Commentary:

At his insisting request, I put the interview up that night, Tuesday march 2, (march 3 in Ireland as it was 1am UTC)

Email, March 3 2020 / Elena Danaan to Stephen Chua

It's streaming now. Are you sure? I'm going to stay surrounding you with bright light. OMG are you sure?

Elena

Email, March 3 2020 /Stephen Chua to Elena Danaan

YES PUT IT PLEASE
thank you...blacking out again

Stephen Chua

TRANSCRIPT OF THE INTERVIEW OF STEPHEN CHUA

-SUPERSOLDIER-AREA 51

Interview by Elena Danaan - March 3 / 2021

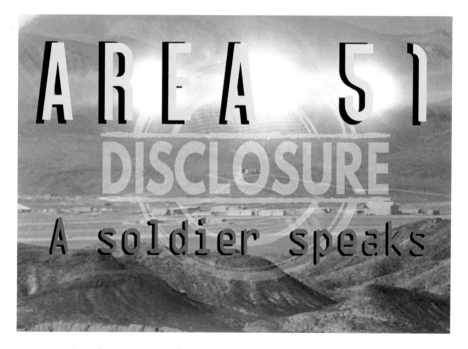

Time has come, when the truth is brought not by the governments, not by the secret services but by the people of Earth themselves. It is no more time to wait for crumbs of disclosure, because the disclosure, it is us. Time has come.

***

The events described by Stephen are not in a chronological order but in the format of a casual conversation, as it happened, with backs and forths in time.

***

Childhood

Stephen:

When I was a very young child, maybe about three, I mean...how innocent can you get! However, somebody tried to kill me, the simple reason being money. He wanted lots of money. So I was hurt, but a being could come and resurrect me right in front of my grandmother. She was so pleased that I was brought back! My clothes were completely scattered but she could see my body being repaired and I was standing straight up, like nothing happened, so she brought me home. That's the first instance. Second instance was, again I was poisoned; I was told by doctors, who told everybody, that I'm not gonna make the night.

And well...this being came down. You know, she took my consciousness, or so, by the hand. We were flying over the rooftops. I could see birds, a couple of little ducks, and my grandparents coming and driving up. And when she brought me back, I related this story to my grandmother. Everybody was astounded, because that's exactly what they saw outside! So these are the events that my grandmother never let me forget. So as I grew up, maybe in a matter of weeks and months, some of these holy men, like priests, and whatever...They do a lot of seances, where they remove all these dark spirits. This is a very common thing, back in the days where I grew up. Children, especially those who were targeted. What they did was just letting me play with a child, and this child was cleaned, that spirit was gone. Not that I did anything special; it's just an energy thing that I worked with, that I guess I carried.

And I've done a lot of them, dozens of them, even the catholic priests took me in because they couldn't handle a spirit that had invaded a child. Anyways, I grew up, I never thought much about it because I just went through life. I find if I come across somebody suffering like this, they just help them, the other beings that were there. Think about it now, there were other beings coming to talk to me; they just sat me down, spoke with me like I was an adult, when I was a child, but I realized these were not humans. They came from somewhere else, because I remember being small and looking up, there was this huge spaceship right above me. Well it was huge, as if you remember, the airlines flying by in the sky, the airliner was flying underneath this ship, and it was just like a little speck, like a little fly compared to the ship. So this ship was massive, and when he went up to the atmosphere, it would just blink in a flashlight and disappear. So definitely not from this Earth.

When it comes to think of it, there have been many many smaller ships, they had come to visit and no idea who they were, but they were not from here. They were you know, a bit like the star wars stuff ships, a lot of them little ones. I never thought much about them and to me, I used to make a lot of sketches in my sketchbook. The teachers said "stop drawing them because your imagination is going crazy!" I was writing and describing a lot of little adventures. I learned to write in fact when I was nine years old. I had my first book then. The school principal saw I had written this massive diaries. As I grew up, I used to travel and to go into the forest. In the jungle, I did a lot of hunting myself, only to have you know, fishing, whatever is just enough of food and people were really astounded that I could even hunt a deer.

Elena:
What age were you?

Stephen:

Maybe my young teens, 12-13 years old. I was doing that already and by the time I was 14 or 15, I was taking people into deep jungles for eco-tours you know, to take pictures of tigers, elephants, giant snakes, whatever...

Entering the military

Stephen:

I entered the arena of some fantastic events, Elena, I just tell the truth. Everybody is asking about my military days, I mean everybody where I came from. You know, I had to go to the military. I didn't think it was the first big extraordinary anything like that; in fact I was so ordinary when I got in there, how I met some people outside I didn't know who they were at first. They had me tested and they went... they say okay, they wanted to send me to ehm...to university in London, England, to get some quality special qualifications. I said okay but first, they say you have to do an IQ test. Would you believe that, I did four of these, four times! Four times because the first time, they just said okay, okay, we had uncertain IQ. Second time, uh yeah, it's not enough because we gotta send you to a higher one and third one, they say they can't assert the result yet, and the fourth time they never gave me an answer. The next week, six officers from the Prime Minister's office came and grabbed me. Prime Minister office, yes! Instantly, well, my life isn't mine anymore.

Elena:

Wow... Could you tell for the audience in which country or area of the world it was, for understanding?

Stephen:

Singapore.

Elena:

Okay, thank you.

Stephen:

The reason why is because I had a type of IQ that was only 11 identified before. I was the 12th one, so instantly this Prime Minister wanted me, as his assets. Can you imagine that! So my life wasn't mine anymore, really. For the next 10 years, I was in the military special forces. I became a sniper. I also had art talents, like the hunting and all that. I was just a little unusual, not quite a normal human. I developed also a kind of um...there's something unusual, see, when I was growing up as a kid, I had ability to use a sword. Never been taught, never been trained, but I had the ability to use a sword. Swordsman, I was very good at it. Even the Kung Fu teacher said he wanted to teach me. He says okay, hit me. I said no, he insisted so I did, and ehm...never heard from him again for the next hour and a half, because I hit him on the head. I mean I was only about eight or nine years old.

And you know, that's very embarrassing for a guy like that. Anybody else, even if it's four or five people attacking me, either with sticks in replacement of a sword, none of them could come anywhere near me right, and I was extremely good at it, so I had no idea where this came from. It's like it's like genetic memory. And also, I had developed a tremendous amount of strength like I was maybe 11 or 12, but I had the strength of an adult. I felt stronger than most adults at that age. You know, there are people who can lift a barrel barrel full of rocks. If one person can't do it, you need to. I could do it myself. Right at that age, it was scary because I didn't look big. I wasn't huge, I didn't look very strong, but I was anyway. That helps in the military.

Banking

Stephen:

Because of where I was, who I was, actually when I started finding out, the old people who was actually my biological grandfather owned a bank. So this is where he taught me banking. I was also a banker at the same time, I mean at the higher level, not the bank teller, like a China Bank officer. So I know what banking is internationally, and the Prime Minister was okay with it because he wanted super intelligent people around him, especially when he's dealing money. So I've been sent to many nations. I was given a lot of authority over many, many things. I told the Prime Minister he could raise my rank anytime he wanted!

Mission against the Khmer Rouge

Stephen:

I reached the rank of colonel at the age of 21. Nobody else in the world has that rank at that young age. However, then I carried myself very well, I spoke very well. I was like a businessmen; nobody questioned me about anything but also, they knew that in the military. Any crazy missions, guess who goes! Of course. Anyway, I was given charge of a contingent of military to hold back the Khmer Rouge over in Thailand. That was encouraging and it's a lot of people, they have a huge army there, and if they have a cross, nothing can stop them you know, the whole region will be under their control.Anyway there was one time, when they started making an attack, I won't go into details of what it did but even though, we had a very small contingent. We didn't turn back.

The entire army continued and then we were gone, but you see, all our weaponry was completely useless forces, very small, but we managed to wipe out their air force. We worked out the floating assets, we wiped out their hardware, the cannons and all of that, so the rest of the army turned around, thankfully. But if they knew what we had left, they would have continued, because our guns, our main guns, we had one shell left, one! Can you imagine that! We fired everything else, we only had one left. Our helicopters were completely dry yeah, no more missiles, nothing else!

But the idea of how to attack them was given like the plan to do; it was like somebody up there giving me the plans, and I had another thing: within 30 seconds, of wondering what to do, because I had no time to wait and not have to ask for permission for anything, just go ahead and do it, "somebody" told me. And uh of course, the king was extremely grateful. Grateful enough to give us a bank branch in Bangkok. It was fine. There are many, many, many other adventures' wonders.

Attempt of assassination of Benazir Bhutto and first encounter with Reptilians

Stephen:

Okay ehm let's get back to this, it's very interesting. They have been used for assassinations. Like sometimes, Singapore is used as a destination for world leaders to come and have a platform to speak, yeah right, but we were always on the lookout for assassins and ehm... Former Prime Minister Benazir Bhutto, the lady from Pakistan, I was assigned to protect her. So me and my team were protecting her, and we were told by the MI-6, British, and CIA in USA, they said there was... they said they knew of an assassin, they were coming to try something.

That time they did, they showed up. I said I was a sniper okay, but the sniper gun I use you really can't use it in the city because it's a 50 caliber and carries explosive shells. It will blow through a tank armor, it's a special type of weapon. I do carry another one, a handgun which has an expanded gas chamber, so we sometimes call it the urban sniper, it's a handgun that's a powerful rifle.

So um we shot the first two, didn't kill them. They shot them again, got them. They were humans except...the third one wasn't. The third one was a little way off on the street, getting ready to fire. This should be for the Prime Minister of Pakistan. I noticed, you know...being being a hunter in the jungle, you notice things. So I sense him, find him, and he realized I'd seen him and he started running. I shot him six times, would you believe! Regular bullets do not penetrate his skin. I know what you gotta say, right!

And it runs very, very fast, and I told my guys, the almighty rest of my team: do not apprehend him because I need something unusual! I caught up with him and I gave him a choice: surrender or die now! Because I switched over the bullets to piercing now and if I used it, he'd be dead. I got a little closer and found his skin was a bit scaly... Okay it looked like a human at long distance, but when you get close, he got very thick darker skin and scaly. It was a hybrid, human-reptilian hybrid. And let me say: extremely strong. He had one more ability, he could uh... hypnotize the person standing in front of him. He was for fighting so we arrested him, but uh you know, when we handed him over, we had no idea where he went. You know, secret stuff okay, but that wasn't the only uh...first.

Commentary:

I could corroborate the visit of Benazir Bhutto in Singapore, in 1995, from the national archives on Singapore Government Agency website (opposite page). So it would be interesting to dig deeper into finding which are the organizations that could employ reptilian hybrids, because this is evidence that Benazir Bhutto knew too much and was opposing the agendas of the Deep State.

NATIONAL ARCHIVES OF SINGAPORE

ABOUT PHOTOGRAPHS   FAQS   ORDERING   CONTACT US

Source:	MINISTRY OF INFORMATION AND THE ARTS (MITA)
Unedited Description Supplied by Transferring Agency:	PRIME MINISTER OF PAKISTAN BENAZIR BHUTTO VISITS THE ORCHID ENCLOSURE AT SINGAPORE BOTANIC GARDENS
Description Edited by NAS:	Pakistani Prime Minister Benazir Bhutto, who is in Singapore for a three-day official visit, arriving at Singapore Botanic Gardens for a tour of the Orchid Enclosure. On the left are Executive Director of National Parks Board Dr Tan Wee Kiat and Minister of State for Health and Education Dr Aline Wong (behind him, partially hidden).
Covering Date:	09/03/1995
Media - Image No:	19990000138 - 0064
Negative No:	CL2229/17/05A
Conditions Governing Access:	Viewing permitted. Use and reproduction only with permission.
Credit Line:	Ministry of Information and the Arts Collection, courtesy of National Archives of Singapore

Do you have more information on this record?

Item added to cart

Processing of requests may require 3-5 working days

+ -

Reptilian on an Air Base

Stephen:

First time I've come across a Reptilian, I was in the air base. There was a time when the Prime Minister of Singapore was being forced, was being asked to do many things that he didn't want to, too bad for his reputation. I noticed when I was walking by on patrol, just a normal trooper, walking by this fenced-up non-secured area. They had these liquid petroleum tanks, giant ones, they supply guests to households, and in the airport and all that. Yeah that's also where the person was, and that was when I was confronted to one of these things. I pulled him out the ground and took the gun away from him, because in that situation you can't fire anything otherwise the whole thing blows up! So I had another hand to hand come back with these guys. He wasn't easiest, easiest guy to take down, but I managed eventually. And then, the whole base is locked down to search for these fellas. I brought in my team and they grabbed him and cuffed him. I told my team: "don't just use those ready handcuffs, you know those, you've got to use those heavy prison ones, these guys are incredibly strong!" Again...he vanished. Yeah, ehm after being arrested, he vanished! So, regular human hybrids are around, and they're not just imagination. They're real.

Elena:

Do you think they were working for the government there, or special organizations, somebody else somewhere else, certainly?

Stephen:

Ehm...I don't know. England, China...

Reptilian hybrid hiding on a military base

Chasing demons

Stephen:
There was a third time, where Thai people were scared after what they said there was a demon running in the place. I know that the case was about drugs, NCI. They send a squadron to go and try and kill something there, but the team never came back.

I was asked to go inside and investigate. I did, and it was run by what they called "the demon", the same thing, the same hybrid, human-reptilian rebuild hybrid. This guy, well...you know my team are all snipers, very, very good ones. You can hold back a thousand people, doesn't matter if they are a kilometer away, you can hold them all back. They can come forward, you take them all down if they're close enough, then they'll get us but when they're far away we have time to get them.

So ehm... that leader was completely surrounded. What he did was, he pulled the old fashioned sword and challenged to battle openly. So I did. A really scary mountain! I wounded his leg, his arm, the other leg and you know what... he didn't die! It's incredible these things, these creatures they're very resilient. It was difficult. Arrived up there the police. When they saw him they just ran away, because they said he's a demon, he's just screaming.

Elena:
Can you describe him a bit more?

Stephen:
Human-like again, very human-like, but heavier stature than normal humans. Thicker bigger bodies, stickier arms and all that.

Naga warrior attacking villagers

Stephen:

The very strong legs are a little bit more extended so they move it really fast, and it's like they can sense your next move. You see, with the training I had, the fighting, you can't sense me because I don't think. I don't think about the next move at all. I'm thinking probably three or four moves ahead so you can't counter that one. You can literally come to the next one here and you think I'm gonna reach that third or fourth move. I will, I may not let me deviate again. So I was trained that way, different way, I'm fighting for energy, very different. The skills (of these beings), again, tough as hell, very very tough skills. You hit it and you find that you, you're hurting, you lose your hands and regular bullets do not penetrate. It's thick, there. You can't pull it out so you need armor-piercing bullets to get through this, through underneath yeah.

Elena:

So that's my question: what I would like to know is how do you... what is the best way to kill them efficiently? Quickly?

Stephen:

I would slash the throat. It is smooth because it has to breathe, otherwise the rest of the bodies are incredibly tough, even the torso. These human hybrids, they do not have a tail. I've seen real Ciakahrrs, they do have a short tail. This one had no tail at all. Okay, yeah there was another incidence. There was this time, in Japan, they had no idea what was going on around the country. There were three of these guys killing people. There are in the country hundreds and hundreds of people, who were shut down completely. Caught one of them, the other two escaped. Then I noticed they were using a Gray saucer. Normally they would sense uh somebody coming.

Elena:

Did you see them beaming into the ship or going into it?

Stephen:

Climbing into the ship. So the ship had landed, the ship was landed okay, discoidal ehm Gray saucer yeah, it's a Gray one, same saucers in Area 51 *(This happened in the 1990's, years after Stephen's stay in Area 51 which was in the 1980's)*. Ehm about Ciakahrrs, where did I see the first one, there's only one time out in Malaysia, West Malaysia and North-East Malaysia, it's very mountainous, it's a very forested mountainous area, and the people were complaining that the children get going missing. And again, we were asked to investigated. So me and my team, seven, we're going to investigate wherever we have a shot. We came to a place where there was a mountain, with a huge cavern underneath, huge! When I say huge, is: a plane could fly into it. But as we approach, I know, you know, I noticed uh... something moving. And a Ciakahrr came out of it! It challenged us, yelled at us, can you imagine our shock!

This being was about nine feet tall, with sharp teeth little steal, in a face growling at us. It was wearing armor, you know, dark skinned, very scary being, and his legs you know, it was like extended, that seems to have another joint, so it has extremely long legs. Actually it looks like a very very powerful being. And he took out his gun... its an energy weapon, and just fired at a rock and you know, the rock just blew up! It's not like it was a small rocket, I mean it was like like a ray about two meters across, but it just blew it right up! It was his gun, it was an energy beam, or energy being used, yeah. So instantly, bang bang, the soldiers that we were trained to be like, we took off, we called ehm to cover, right, and then...more of them showed up! And started firing!

Malaysia has the world's largest cave systems and as a matter of fact, some of them are large enough to allow a plane fly into it, such as the Sarawak chamber (above) or the Deer Cave (below).

Stephen meeting with a Reptilian in a Malaysian cave.

Stephen:

So we fired back but my guys were just complaining; can't get them at all, they keep bouncing around because then, the moment before you can squeeze the trigger, they got out of kind of a position. You couldn't fire at them, you can't figure them at all. Regular arrays anywhere, regular arrays didn't do anything to them you know, they didn't care. They just...stood there, let the bullets hit them and bounce off their armor and their bodies or whatever. They just weren't afraid of us. That was until I used my gun, because of the 60 uranium explosive rods, and that made them shake a bit because those rods should kill them. However, they move so fast, we just couldn't hit them but we did carry one more thing. I did carry one more thing because I'm authorized to do that. You've got a bazooka, like a weapon fires, not in the bazooka, not the regular, basically; the warhead is actually what we call neutron device.

Elena:

Oh wow okay, it's nuclear!

Stephen:

Nuclear, yeah. Okay, I carried one of them. I don't use it sometimes because it's dangerous, yeah, but in that situation... We fire on it, we fired the device into the cave. An almighty blaster! And we ran, we ran for dear life up there! Because I mean we were completely outgunned by these guys, their weapons were just incredible. You can't hide behind anything, they just keep blowing it up you know, even big rocks are just blowing up! Anyway we ran, ran and ran, and ran, and didn't stop, but we did send a helicopter search the next day. I found the mountain had completely collapsed and there was no more stories about using children after that.

Elena:

So they abandoned the place and they collapsed the mountain themselves, to block the entrance of the cave?

Stephen:

No I don't think so, I think they ran to the back, they ran deeper inside because the neutron bomb would have collapsed the mountain. Oh yeah, yeah the blast would be powerful and enough. So they gave up and they ran away, and missing children was finished. I guess they abandoned the outpost. They were discovered. That was a very threatening situation because it took us a long time to get around there, so what the hell did we just encounter with no idea, no idea such beings existed! So it was quite frightening at first. There are many other situations with the other friendly ET's. They're not always so nasty.

Elena:

I would like to hear about these ones too.

Stephen:

Well, friendly as in you know, like the first case where I was resurrected, right there, with another kid. Another time when there was this holy man sitting by the river, I decided I wanted to go fishing in the river so I mean he gave me a shotgun! When he started talking to me he was curious, he was asking about what I thought about this fish what did I think about little things, talking about normal everyday things. And then he gave me a little bit of advice and said:
-*"there's more to come in your life".*
I had no idea what he meant so he said:
-*"be prepared, it will get very very bad, but you will survive it somehow",* he said.
-*Thanks a lot,* I replied.
But what were they, just a kind of warning, at the time?

Commentaries:

NAGA AND CIAKAHRR

The Mahabharata was the first text to introduce the Nagas. This epic saga is believed to have been written, for its older pieces, around 400 BC, depicting events that could have happened around the 8th or 9th century BC. In the ancient Hindu scriptures, the "Naga" or "Nagi" were serpent gods who dwell in caves and underground tunnels in the Himalayas, the underworld "Naga-Loka", or "Patala-Loka". They can occasionally shape-shift and take human form, and are sometimes called: " The Serpent People". Traditions say that they could fly around in magical machines. The underground cities were lit by "magical stones" and treasures carefully guarded by the Serpent People. Sacrificial rituals devoted to these supernatural beings have been taking place throughout south Asia for at least two thousand years.

In India there are a large number of secret underground cities which were, according to ancient texts, used by a Reptilian beings. I may cite two examples such as the Kugai Murugan cave systems, for instance, where lived a Reptilian hybrid named Surah Padman. This is mentioned in ancient Indian texts and some locals claimed that there was a cave used in the past by Reptilians. Indeed, a vast web of caves linked by tunnels runs deep beneath the surface. We can find at the entrance some altars with fresh offerings, and little cavities in the walls for oil lamps, some kind of rituals are still performed in this place. Several long tunnels lead deep down into the Earth. According to the ancient texts: Surah Padman was not human but half Naga, because his father, named Badr Naga, was an alien. It has been documented multiple times in ancient Indian texts, that Nagas lived in underground cities and used secret entrances. Another evidence is the Ellora caves, where we can find carvings of Naga reptilian beings near the entrance. A steep rectangular tunnel about 1 Ft wide and 40 Ft deep, leads access to deeper levels. The tunnel takes a right angle turn to proceed underground.

The Patala-Loka and the Naga-Loka are underground places populated by different beings. The "Lokas" (mystical kingdoms) are typically divided into seven upper worlds, or Vyahritis, and seven lower worlds collectively referred to as the Sapta Adho-Loka, or Patalas. Patala-Loka, the seventh and lowest of levels, is filled with resplendent palaces of crystal, beautifully ornamented with precious gems. Is the Naga-Loka the place where Reptilian extraterrestrial dwell in an underground web of caves? Is the Patala-Loka a web of deeper underground facilities built and equipped with a technology based on crystals? Could these "palaces of crystal" have been built by the same people from the Intergalactic Confederation, named Pa-Taal? When I visited one of their motherships, what surprised me at first was the architecture made of crystal, either as a material or as incorporated clusters. Can we reasonably draw a link to the Pa-Taal, the intergalactic founder races who claim having an old underground residence in the Himalayas?

We find the name "Shikhar" in Sanskrit, which stands for: "Hunter / Predator". As I was taught by Thor Han in early 2020, The Naga and Ciakahrr are two very dangerous Reptilian races who have been operating on Earth for a long period of time. Both are related but they have two different stories regarding the visits and the occupation of this planet. Andromedan contactee Alex Collier mentioned these beings already in the early 1990's, in his book "Defending Sacred Ground".

These beings are originally from another dimension but they settled in the star systems of the Draconis constellation, named as such for a probable reason. The Ciakahrr are the overlord class and the Naga the warrior cast. The difference is the presence of tail, horns and wings in the Ciakahrr elite class. The Naga's appearance varies in color, but they will often have striped markings. All social casts and racial types are skilled deceivers and shapeshifters. As it is not part of the main topic of this book, I am inviting you to discover more detailed information on these beings, their society, activities and misdeeds on Earth in my publication: "A Gift From The Stars", and in "Defending Sacred Ground" from Alex Collier.

Naga and Ciakahrr have been for a very long time heavily involved in the traffic of human children mainly as a food resource and galactic trade, under the shameful cover up and horrendous collaboration of the Deep State goverments. So the accounts of Stephen Chua's experience facing Reptilians in caves, with disappearence of children involved, matches perfectly, in all details, with the facts above.

AREA 51

Stephen:

Now a lot of people ask me about area 51. You know, it was in the early 80s', some time ago. I had a very special ability. I was tested and they found that I could project gamma vibrations, detectable gamma. You know, you have a measuring device and they'll detect the gamma rays effect. They could actually measure my waves outside of my body, so I could affect things that way. I know they've been used sometimes. I walk by the television side and sometimes the television goes off or do something funny. So since I knew that I had this gamma ability, there were some... not CIA but higher circuit service people... they asked if I could be brought to area 51 for testing, for development. When the Prime Minister heard that it was to do with aircrafts, he said: *"Okay, only for two weeks, so we lend you to them."*

Elena:

So you said it wasn't the CIA... was it another Secret Services you didn't know anything about?

Stephen:

No, much higher up, somewhere dark, yeah, much darker... something to do with space, whatever aerospace developments, and whatever. Anyway, I was brought there and like, you see, for two very intense weeks. I was assigned two guards, two humans. They carried guns. They didn't carry the regular ehm... bullet weapons. They carried energy weapons. I also asked them *"why did you carry these?"* They answered: *"Why do I have them, to keep the ETs away from you."* And so, I didn't know at the time, but I could see this now, that I know that the Gray Alliance are really nasty people. Nasty beings... that's why. Because there are a lot of little ones running around, like little robots androids. And there's the Kiily-Tokurt, tall, light, and I did see one or two of these. And the Maytre, actually. Horrible... they had horrible attitudes.

Elena:

So can you describe all the races you've seen there, in area 51, interacting with humans?

Stephen:

So well yeah, the most of the interactions are by telepathy. You have one assigned officer that is telepathically inclined to interpret what these people are trying to communicate. In fact, if there's a scientist there, you have this telepathic guy. With the scientists as well outside the Area 51. The parameters of the security is incredibly tight. Inside, it's more fun in there; the humans can use at least a lot of jokes and they push each other around a lot, all fun and games and stuff. One day I saw this object flying vertical. I realized oh okay, what's this floating in the mid air there? It was some craft construct by the Gray ones. A form I don't recognize, but it's floating there, and also that's pretty small, no bigger than 10 meters across.

Stephen:

But there was one there ,also, like at least 50 meters across, and it's saucer shape and it's floating. It wasn't touching the ground and the beings they go up and down this beam thing, up or down, and that's the one we rode in actually, later on.

Elena:

O yeah you told me *(in a zoom conversations listed in this book)* you were onboard one of these! Could you describe the different races that you saw over there, so you said to me the Maytre, Kiily-Tokurt...

Stephen:

The Maytre I can remember them very well, yes, very clearly. Mainly because of the bloody activity that they carry. They're very, very, very vicious looking, that they could seem to be aloof. The Maytre wore that very dull bluish type of coat or jumpsuit you know, body covering, it must be some kind of armor type material as well. The little Grays they wore nothing, they just ran around, They stink though!

Elena:

The little Grays stink yes, absolutely.

Stephen:

You can always tell them before they arrive, they stink! *(laughs)*

Elena:

You smell them before you see them yeah! It is like a smell like rotten a bit?

Stephen:

Really a bad toilet, yes. And it gets just especially bad when there's a bunch of them. If there's a bunch of them in a small room, the humans what they do is they turn on the exhaustion full on!

Elena:

And this, as we speak about them, these little small Grays, what were their tasks? Do you think they were assigned to certain work there, or a certain purpose?

Stephen:

Yes they seem to be doing the same thing over and over and over again.

Elena:

Which was?

Stephen:

You see them sometimes adjusting pieces of equipment, sometimes assembling some little pieces of equipment or organizing a panel of some kind, and always after that is done, a tall Gray or a Maytre will take over. They're like little servants. And they never smile.

Elena:

Do you think they could have been like synthetic or real biological beings?

Stephen:

They seemed like biological but I didn't feel any auras from them. I had the ability to see auras, you know.

Elena:

That's interesting! So they were assigned to taller Grays you said, isn't it.

Stephen:

Yes.

Elena:

These taller Grays were they Maytra, Kiily-Tokurt or another species?

Stephen:

Ehm I don't see any other species, only those three.

Elena:

Okay, can you describe the Kiily-Tokurt as you you saw them, please?

Stephen:

Oh yes there was, well, like Grays but tall, much taller, longer necks, skinny, and the females have very long hair.

Elena:

Very long hair... and the color of the skin?

Stephen:

Yeah the color of skin is, I don't know why they call him white; it's more like death, somebody had died, definitely! That color is not very pleasant, it's like you take a dead person out of the freezer, you know. It does sort of reminds me of a white dolphin.

Elena:

Yeah okay, and their eyes?

Stephen:

Rather tilted, almond shaped, and very piercing because they communicate through telepathy. And I could tell that they were not used... to being polite. You know they say okay I want to eat you, its okay to tell you how I will eat you, I want this, I want that thing...

Elena:

Were their face human or they had more like a traditional Gray face?

Stephen:

Elongated, like you know you have a barbie doll, and you slap it flat.

Elena:

Very good picture, yeah! Do you think that some people could call them the Tall Whites?

Stephen:

Yeah ehm... They were referred to us as Tall Whites in there, and the guys, there were humans there, were very wary of them, because they like to go into mind control.

Elena:

What do you think the purpose of the Kiily-Tokurt was, residing in area 51? Their work, their job?

Stephen:

Well I think they seemed to be doing two things that I noticed. One was: some scientists were being instructed on building, you know they wanted to build more deals of those spaceships, this way or that way, and telling the scientists they want this, they want the engineers to do engineering, in that way.. and another thing is: some of the others will come and offer technical advice on... the humans were developing a floating device, for example, so these engineers and scientists were being instructed then, on the energies required. Some were instructing, some were so I guess... it is to do with um getting every resources to build something and in return, they're getting instruction on technology.

Elena:

They were residing in the Area 51?

Stephen:

Yes, they had their own area.

Elena:

Was it buildings or underground?

Stephen:

Underground. They prefer always living underground, which is very strange.

Elena:

So would you say they were giving instructions and a consultancy in alien technology to the personnel of area 51?

Stephen:

Yes.

Elena:

What were they getting in exchange?

Stephen:

I think they... I can tell you this: I don't know if it's because they're lazy, they don't build industrial stuff. Industrial stuff is something that Earth does very well. Current people do it very well. They don't, they need somebody to build their hardware for them. So they would ask us to develop it for them, to do whatever they wanted.

Elena:

Do you think they had a more personal secret purpose to it?

Stephen:

Oh yes, definitely.

Elena:

Something that they were doing in the undergrounds and the other the bases, that humans were not allowed to interfere?

Stephen:

Much.

Elena:

What do you think they were doing?

Stephen:

Ehm I don't think there were any human exper-iments down there, because area 51 is more mechani-cal. You know, in development of weapons and such. So what was the big thing over there was energy emissions. So I mean, this is where the Earth people, our people, try to transfer this technology to their own aircraft. And this is where I came in. So what they do, I don't know if you noticed outside of area 51, sometimes there's a whole squadron of F-15s sitting outside. They're mostly experimental planes. I think the little history I had with these, what I was told was this: they had a lot of vol-unteer pilots, very good ones, to develop fly-by-thought planes. However, normally, humans do not generate a lot of gamma projections outside the body. They don't do it naturally. It's inside your brain, you can have it blowing up, but to project it that's not quite normal. So what they do is they inject this pilot with some kind of a serum that over-activates the brain, and they go flying out and they come back. Do it too often, the brain turns into mush. Many pilots died. The brain just disintegrates. So they were running out of pilots and they didn't want anymore their pilots to die, so... when they found me they tried to have a different approach. So what they did was they trained me to fly a plane, flying an F-15. You've gotta do it very fast, but I do learn very quickly because like I learned to fly a helicopter over the weekend.

Elena:

So how was that working? You were in a seat in the plane, and were there electrodes or something? Tell me the details please.

F-15 Eagle

Stephen:

Oh, this crazy helmet! These things were sticking all over the place. And there's a bunch of equipment behind, so what they've done is they had ripped out the back seat, this is a F-15f, it's a two seated. I was sitting in front, I was the obvious pilot, and the co-pilot seat will be ripped out and all the equipment is there, behind me. But in the meantime I was wearing this helmet with things sticking out all over the place, like a giant virus *(laugh)*. So, I would take off, and then a lot of practice flights, and then they put me into maneuvers.

Elena:

How do you that? You just think about the place you want the plane to go?

Stephen:

So initially, it was flying by hand, right, and later on I started to use stuff to be hands off and let the instruments take over, ran by thought. What advantage that is: after a while, not immediately but after a while, you see when you're doing it manually it could take half a second to go through a maneuver and a sequence of half seconds for different maneuvers. So when you're fighting an enemy plane, doing maneuvers and all that, you know several seconds go by, and by them the missile might hit you. However, if all of these can be done in half a second combined, what have you got: an incredibly powerful machine, faster than anything and anybody can imagine. So that's the result. In fact I got it down to about 0.2 seconds. Thought is still a lot faster. Like I could roll, aim fire and roll back again, in a matter of 0.2 seconds. Oh and then I can even switch over to a different weapon while I'm doing all that. Which is uh quite unheard of.

Stephen:

There's no one able probably to do it manually. So the engineers were really overjoyed that it can be done. Because they had it on record right, this year: now there is another plane that is that kind of rocket. You can do a lot of things with future weaponry. I don't know but for some reason they stopped the program.

Elena:

Maybe they did not want to kill all the pilots. They better stopped! Well nothing can stop them, I mean I don't know, these people have other sorts of ethics. Well a different one anyway.

Stephen:

Well anyway, that was ehm... fun. So at the end of it all, they gave me a patch to call you you can fly what we call an F-15 Eagle, that's the plane. So they could see "Eagle driver" on the patch *(laugh)*.

The F-15 Eagle Driver patch

Elena:

So you have been on board a ship, a Gray alien ship? Tell me about that.

Stephen:

Yes. All right. We were invited. This was not the Grays idea, it was one of the generals' idea. They wanted to give me a ride, and show something. They do short trips here to there, so I said okay, sounds like fun! So my guards and his guards and so maybe there were eight or nine of us, humans, going up. It's kind of a weird feeling, like being in that energy thing going up, initially, prickling all over *(laugh)*. I was lifted from the ground into the ship.

Elena:

Oh yeah you were lifted by an energy beam into the ship!

Stephen:

Yeah, weird feeling. And we were told okay, this is the sitting area, you must sit here, and observe the Grays functioning.

Elena:

It was the little ones?

Stephen:

The little ones were all on the panels, I think they were just like six or seven of them, on the panels working, and there was this Kiily-Tokurt standing right in the front, making sure that everybody knows that he's the captain, you know that kind of thing ehm anyway. So when the ship started to move, it was wobbly. It wobbled. *(laughs)* A couple of little Grays and the captain turned on me, he looked at me and he said: *"Stop it!"* I said: *"What?"*

Elena:
The Kiily-Tokurt just told you *"stop it"* !*(Laughters)*

Stephen:
I just looked at him and said:
-Stop what? (laugh).
I wasn't afraid of him either. You know, the generals were laughing, laughing, and they said to me:
-You're not afraid? (laugh).
-Why would I be? I said *(laugh).*
There's the reason why. The generals started to say:
-Well, what's wrong?
-It is interfering with our controls! The Kiily-tokurt replies.
Ah... how am I interested in the controls? It's because I'm focusing on the panels and they're sensitive!

(laughters)

Elena:
Oh my god! So if you were allowed, you could have taken over the ship, and navigated it!

Stephen:
Because the gamma projections from me were very strong, it was stronger than theirs.

Elena:
So in fact that is very interesting, because I've heard some ships, some of their technology, it's just the ship that is plugged and attuned to the DNA or the brain waves of the pilots, but obviously there are some ships that are not, and anybody hat has the ability can pilot them. So then like this one, anyway.

Stephen:
Yeah, I was surprised. I said *"Ok..."* Woops...

Stephen reprimended by the Kiily-Tokurt captain.

Elena:

Woops! *(laughters)* What was their uniforms, the Kiily-Tokurt? Did they have a uniform?

Stephen:

Ehm I wouldn't call it a uniform. It's more like a "coverall" they're wearing on Earth. They would seem to be wearing a different one than the others that come and go from space, coming down, those are probably the uniforms but those on Earth, I think it's a different one. They wear something different.

Elena:

Have you seen any symbols or insignias on their uniforms, all these Ets?

Stephen:

The Kiily-Tokurts no, I don't remember the insignias, but I do remember the Maytras: the triangles right with the stripes.

Elena:

Ah that's it, like a little triangle with three stripes?

Stephen:

Yeah, that's it! Yeah they all wear the same thing.

Elena:

Now please, tell us about the the Maytra. So what can you tell us about them?

Stephen:

Not a lot because they were being kept away from me, but they were interested in who I was. They did ask questions, they even kind of come to approach, but my guards would point the guns up and say *"go!"* And they didn't come any closer.

Elena:

Were they... how was their general behavior, attitude, the Maytre?

Stephen:

Rude. Vicious. They can't seem to be without hate, or growl. Something like... think of a tiger.

Elena:

Yeah, like a tiger energy, very aggressive, aren't they.

Stephen:

Yes, very. Very dangerous. You can tell from the energy that they were aggressive.

Elena:

Were they smelling as well?

Stephen:

Some. Some, yes. It's like a mold type of smell.

Elena:

Were they residing on the base, I mean probably underground?

Stephen:

Yes, they had their own spots.

Elena:

Were they getting on with the other Grays, like the Kiily-Tokurt?

Stephen:

No, they ordered them. They're not...they don't seem like allied or buddies; they just order them.

Elena:

They tolerate each other?

Stephen:

Yeah, and very often they come very close to a fight, actually.

Elena:

Between Maytre and Kiily-Tokurt yes, I believe that.

Stephen:

Not-unusual.

Elena:

What do you think was the purpose of the presence of the Maytre in Area 51?

Stephen:

They came to take something. Take something, not really give. Maybe there's something they had planned, they promised to exchange the humans, I don't know.

Elena:

Do you think they were the ones who made agreements with the government in the 1950s ?

Stephen:

I don't think in the 1950's, it is something more recent.

Elena:

Do you think they were taking people, using humans?

Stephen:

I think so, because they were there, and their attitude...you know, when they saw me, they wanted to approach, and they wanted to know me, without even asking, to just come.

Elena:

They want something and they take it, don't they...

Stephen:

Yes... And you can see that the other guys were ready to shoot at them.

Elena:

And I suppose there was... but was there an exchange? With I mean, what you said, that they didn't give anything...

Stephen:

I didn't see them give anything.

Elena:

So it was more: they were here and nobody had to say anything because everybody was scared of them?

Stephen:

People were afraid of them. And they carried one more thing: they carried an energy weapon as well. They had a packet, something, and they carried an energy type weapon that there's like a bit of lightning. You fire it out, so whoever's at the end of that thing is gonna be fried. I saw them use it once, on some equipment, and they just... because they were unhappy with the piece of equipment they fried the front of the equipment. Incredible! They had incredible power carrying with them.

Elena:

Very impressive. What about the interdimensional side of these beings, have you experienced they had activity on other dimensional planes? Were they able to shift dimensionally or modify the fabric of space-time?

Stephen:

Yes. One time, I noticed that the Maytre, they had their own meeting with their own people from somewhere else. There was also a portal, you know. I could see that the room, the area where they were, clear air, and then there was this watery like uh... you think they're round, and you step through it.

Elena:

Is it like in the movie "Stargate", yo would say ?

Stephen:

Not quite that elaborate. You can see wave-forms, they are energy changing, so they can step back and forth from that. I guess it's a sort of like... more or less from the beings on the other side.

Elena:

So there were beings coming through this portal from the other side?

Stephen:

Yeah they came through or something, then they went back.

Elena:

Were they all Maytre, or other species as well?

Stephen:

Maytre. I stayed there one time and it's like, okay I'm staying away from you guys *(laughs)*.

Elena:

Yes, you would anyway, yeah! What about the different ships? Could you say they had each different types of ship? Different shapes?

Stephen:

Yes, different shapes. I cannot really describe exactly what they looked like, but using the Grays ship as as a basis, they actually looked very similar. But I noticed that the Maytre ships have a lot more energy; they glow a lot more. And also, you can feel the energy more, you come too closely you feel that it might fry you or something.

The Maytre's portal

Elena:

Yes, it's the energy field around the ship, that you can't approach. Have you learned anything about this technology, how it was working, this energy field, for instance?

Stephen:

The very basics, I did. And there's one more reason why the humans keep me away because I pick it up, because for those things I'm very fast *(laughs)*. After this episode, I went back to my base. With pilots from the old aircraft, I developed um... I made something. A floating device. It's small, but it would handle uh... I don't know how many hundred times its own weight. And the Vatican heard about it, and they wanted it.

Elena:

The Vatican wanted it? It was a floating device like... anti-gravity, or another technology?

Stephen:

Anti-gravity. That was very, very stable.

Elena:

Was it alien technology or retro-engineered?

Stephen:

Me, I did it.

Elena:

You did it! You manufactured this device, you put it together!

Stephen:

From understanding what was going on and I put it together.

Elena:

And you understood it from a ship, for instance?

Stephen:

Yes, but I wasn't going to let them have it. So I decided to toil it apart *(laughs).*

Elena:

So, it was someone from the Vatican... I know you told me this story before but I would like you to tell the audience. Someone from the Vatican heard about this device, they wanted it, they sent someone who tried to get it from you, isn't it?

Stephen:

Yes.

Elena:

I would like you to say the name of this person, because for anybody who has read my book, I mentioned this person with Area 51...

Stephen:

Yeah he's Dr Jenkins.

Elena:

Thank you, thank you... So ehm you destroyed, you dismantled this device, that nobody could have it.

Stephen:

That's right.

Elena:

Would you be able to make it again?

Stephen:

Right now, I do not know if I can remember it, because in the meantime, all those years, I suffered several strokes, because of the stress. And um you know, much of my memory is... I've come across situations where my memories were wiped. It must have been several times because I can feel like...there were empty spaces in my head, but every... every so often, I get flashes of returning memory, which is wonderful because you know, holes in your head isn't good.

Elena:

No, no... What do you think these holes in your head are due to? Damage from all of these experiments and work, or alien intervention?

Stephen:

I think the alien intervention.

Elena:

Do you think they wiped your memory on purpose?

Stephen:

Yes.

Elena:

Who did that?

Stephen:

Who did that I do not know exactly, my guess is, I know that one situation would be from the Maytre. One of them, at least. There's more, I know.

Elena:

They didn't want you to remember what happened there.

Stephen:

They didn't want me to remember what happened to me, I mean one of them had possessed me ehm... recently. He attacked me but I've thrown him off, with help from friends. It wasn't easy because my whole body was covered with infections. They did that because they wanted to well...

first, take down my energy, make me helpless and give up. But you see, I will not give up my mind!

Elena:

No! And they are still bothering you and attacking you since all these years?

Stephen:

Yes, they are.

Elena:

You're still fighting.

Stephen:

I've learned to fight back, recently, and I do know one thing though: I have an ability of end-to-end combat. I've never been defeated in any end-to-end combat.

Elena:

They fear you.

Stephen:

I look how big they are, I've always come on top *(laughs)*.

Elena:

You are very brave, and that is amazing. There was a question before we go on, on this subject. When you were working at Area 51, who were your human bosses, I mean what institution?

Stephen:

Oh, ehm...that space agency that the US has. It's dark... The problem with that one is, it's dark, also linked to the Vatican, which is the part I do not like because I run into situations with the Vatican that I was really... I was really shocked at the horrors... that they do things like that.

Like I had a mission with going to Bhutan to save a village, with Gurkharas in the whole regime of Gurkhara. We didn't know he was the french foreign legion working with for the Vatican, stealing artifacts. We stopped them. Well by then half the village had been killed, unfortunately. So ehm... you see, doing all these things, it's no wonder that for decades after, they were coming up to me still, trying to assassinate me. Even recently, you know, when my child was growing up, they tried to kidnap my son. But really, you know, you hear the story about trying to steal a cub from a lioness, no chance! Yeah but for 20 years I was fighting assassins, coming in from nowhere. So life wasn't all that peaceful. Imagine the stress I had to go through.

Elena:

So since you left Area 51, when you left, were you threatened not to speak of it, I suppose?

Stephen:

Yes, ordered not to speak, but the Prime Minister said: "Talk about it, I want to hear!"

Elena:

So you told the Prime Minister in Singapore about your experience?

Stephen:

The Prime Minister and the higher military. You have to tell them, I can't shut up, I'm walking around with that Eagle Driver pilot patch, I mean everybody wants to know *(laughs)*. I walked around with, so it's you know... a lot of people got very interested! How did you get it! I also got a Gurkha sword.

Elena:

This is fascinating. What else do you remember, about what you witnessed in area 51?

Stephen:

Yes, memories do come back. The floors can move.. huge slabs can be redrawn, the ships can go down, sometimes, underneath where we are walking. It's very huge ships underneath.

Elena:

Oh you mean that the floor slides open and the ships go down, and there's a facility under?

Stephen:

Yes, and then we need the tunnels, like from a mountain into this mountain here, there are tunnels. There are more tunnels underneath than there are buildings on top. And many levels down. One place there, went on 10 levels.

Elena:

What's going on in these undergrounds?

Stephen:

Weapons research, technologies, it's mostly mechanical, electronics. It's not an issue. There are things floating by, even if there wouldn't be anybody control it...

Elena:

And would you say that the aliens are walking around, with the people, with the employees of the base?

Stephen:

No, they have generally their own area. There's a cold mingling area, what they call the working areas, it's where they come and go. Other than that, they don't have their "buddy-buddy" relaxed atmosphere when they're off work. It's dangerous. It's dangerous for the humans.

Elena:

Yes, so they don't like humans, either the Kiily-Tokurt or the Maytre. We know that but it's really important to explain to the audience. So the Maytre are there, we don't really know what they do, but they abduct humans, that's it? Have you suspected that they were working with taking humans, but nobody really knows?

Stephen:

Yes, because you see, with the teleportable technology, they grab somebody and nobody's gonna know.

Elena:

Yeah... do they teleport people just like this, do you think?

Stephen:

I think they have an agreement not to do that I think. Because they need other beings to build things from them.

Elena:

Yes, so they need not to be too horrible!

Stephen:

I've seen them take more deals of stuff, heavy stuff that'd just been created by the humans, delivered to them, they carry and go through the portal, and they take it away with them. I've seen that happen.

Elena:

And the Kiily-Tokurt are there for slave work or mechanical, build stuff, what would you say the main purpose of their presence is?

Stephen:

Really it was us who built things for them. Unfortunately, it's military weapons based.

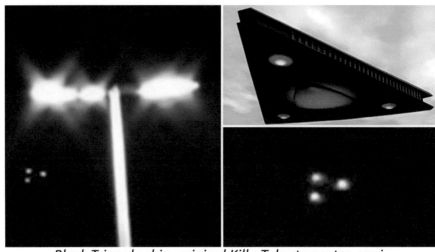

Black Triangle ship, original Killy-Tokurt or retro-engineered.

Stephen:

I can tell that they might be creating some kind of armor or some kind of gun, or some kind of a firing module and like you know, if you go to a battleship on Earth, you see turrets of guns. They had their own version of it, much smaller. But there's a version of it that they put on the ships.

Elena:

Have you seen the triangular black ships?

Stephen:

Yes, they had a triangular ship.

Elena:

That's Kiily-Tokurt.

Stephen:

And they insist in keeping that ship underground.

Elena:

Yes, that's the Kiily-Tokurt, isn't it, that have these black triangular ships.

Stephen:

They like to have it underground.

Elena:

They don't want humans near them?

Stephen:

Yes.

Elena:

They don't want to give the technology.

Stephen:

Anyway, they have this energy thing around them all the time. You really don't want to approach the ship anyway. And whoever human wants to get on board, they get to wear a special suit. Not my cup of tea *(laughs)*.

Elena:

No! Well if they're not friendly, you think twice before getting on board, isn't it!

Stephen:

Yes, I wouldn't go onboard with them even though the ship is empty! I wouldn't go on board because I don't know what the program is.

Elena:

Yeah you want to be sure to be able to get out! *(laughters)* Wow these are amazing things.

Stephen:

The friendly ship I saw, it's a very unusual ship. It's not even like a ship, it's more like a shuttle.

Elena:

Which ones?

Stephen:

Ehm more like a shuttle, like a small bus.

Elena:

Who used this ship?

Stephen:

I have no idea, they didn't tell us, my senses tell it's from friendly ETs. It was just there, anybody could approach and touch it, even.

Elena:

So it would be a fourth species that you didn't see, that would be there using this ship, this bus-shuttle-like?

Stephen:

It was set aside, because it seems the humans didn't pay any attention to it. Which I think it's kind of surprising because I think...my sense is that it's got even higher technology than the other ones, much, much higher. It's a very responsive ship, it is conscious, like if I approach it, it sort of moves a little bit. Which is ehm...I found a little unusual. And you get a sense that it is alive, awake... I do not know whose ship that is. Maybe it was given to them, but they didn't make use of it.

Elena:

Or maybe they took it from somewhere else, or captured this ship and... who knows!

Stephen:

Maybe, but the funny things is, it is a friendly ship.

Elena;

Yes, you felt it was from a friendly species. Maybe it was captured and brought there? Who knows...

Stephen:

Maybe as a gift. I mean if this technology is a gift, that's non-nuclear. A benevolent ET would want you to figure it out.

Elena:

Have you heard about some ties between Area 51 and Wright-Patterson bases in Ohio?

Stephen:

I heard about the underground tunnels, and they actually have trains going back and forth. Because sometimes I saw a bunch of people in the mountains but they didn't come up from the surface. Where did they come from...

Elena:

Yes, that's the big web of underground connecting all the the military bases, the DUMBs and everything,. Wow.

Stephen:

Yeah I didn't know but I don't know if it's like human experiments that they have underground Area 51; is mostly mechanical weaponry, energy, digital, and there's lots and lots of computer stuff.

Elena:

Were they working also on mind control devices?

Stephen:

Mind control devices is very, very common. It's like in the offices, the modules, you get a lot of robots, or something with humans wearing all these crazy devices on their heads, and instruments are always running.

Elena:

So are there humans walking around with these devices on their head?

Stephen:

Not walking around, they stay inside. They are attached to the system but they do have what we call you know, this space centrifuge where they test, where they train you to take G-forces and all the stuff in there, between the humans.

Elena:

Do you think there are humans who are taken in space, off-world, to go to other planets? To work with these ETs somewhere else ?

Stephen:

Oh yes. I've met a few of them, that they say they just come back from Mars. It was like... is that possible? That time I didn't understand, and so I asked them: do you ever go back to Earth? No they're slaves, they work as slaves. If they don't work they get thrown outside and they won't last two minutes.

Elena:

So you met humans, military personnel, coming back from Mars.

Stephen:

I wouldn't call them military personnel, they're more... the more technical people.

Elena:

Technical people coming back from Mars, saying that there are facilities there, where humans are used as slaves?

Stephen:

Yes.

Elena:

And who are the slave-masters?

Stephen:

Yeah I asked them that: *"who controls you?"* They told me that there are a lot of these little Gray ones running around, with little guns, energy guns, but the scary ones are once in a while these Reptilian guys, they come around.

Elena:

Reptilians!

Stephen:

Reptilians, yeah. Some Reptilian ones come around, and those are scary ones.

Elena:

And the little Grays work for the reptilians?

Stephen:

Yes. If the little Grays do something wrong, the Reptilians rip their heads off.

Elena:

So humans are sent to Mars to these bases, as basically a slave force, slaves who work for them.

Stephen:

Yes because they are technically building things, humans are extremely good.

Elena:

Okay, so they employ humans there.

Stephen:

The other races are not good for these sort of things.

Elena:

So the first missions to Mars, it's just a cover-up to make people believe that we are going to build facilities on Mars? But in fact they are here since a long time, isn't it?

Stephen:

They're talking a lot of nonsense, really. What they told me was how they bring equipment you know, some sometimes they require heavy equipment. There are places on the Earth where sometimes there's an explosive effect and things that can be blown into space. So that's what they do, they put it on special containers, bring it to that place on the ocean or whatever it is, and let it blow out into space. What they do is they hook their ships to the whole container and grab them and then bring them to Mars.

Elena:

Do you think that's what they call the "jump rooms"? To go to Mars? People have told about that, there are like places on Earth where there are... it's like portal and people are teleported to Mars? Would you think it's the same thing?

Stephen

The generals mentioned about working within this lab to Mars it transports several people at the same time, but for larger numbers they need a ship.

Elena:

Yes, it makes sense.

Stephen:

And most of these people, the stories they told me about traveling to Mars on the ship wasn't the most pleasant, because those few hours, those few hours riding that ship, life support isn't all that great and very unpleasant. And it's dangerous too, because if you're ever thrown outside the environment of the facilities, there you die in minutes. That's why everybody is very compliant; you don't work you die.

Elena:

Well, you're confirming a lot of things that I was told, and this is quite mind-blowing. Did you hear them talking about the Moon?

Stephen:

Ehm not quite. What happened, I don't know, there's a lot of activity, so...

Commentaries:

Here are excerpts of my repertoire of alien races in "A Gift From The Stars"-2020. When we recorded this session, Stephen hadn't read my book yet. Below are extraterrestrial races potentially fitting descriptions given by Stephen in Area 51. Let us start by the small Grays:

DO-HU (Dow)

Do-Hu

The "Do-Hu" left their home planet in the Zeta Reticuli system in search for a new home. They were captured and assimilated by the Nebu and genetically altered for servitude. The Do-Hu are a hive-consciousness.

This species was originally a cross between reptiloid and botanic genetics. They are cousins with the Solipsi Rai. Their telepathic skills are phenomenal, in particular when it comes to deceive Terran abductees. The Orion and Ciakahrr Empires made of the Do-Hu a group of harmful scavengers at their service. They are sent by their masters on genetic alteration programs towards undeveloped worlds, in order to prepare the ground for invasion, as they did with Terra. Years 1953, 1955, 1957, the Do-Hu motherships arrived in orbit of Terra and took place under the Oceans. This group of Do-Hu was very active on Earth, responsible for abductions. They did their job coldly and without much emotion, of which they have been deprived.

ZETA RETICULI or RETICULANS

Zeta-Reticul Small Grays or Shamtbahali

114

The heart of their hive-culture is on the Xrog twin-planets. Small Grays often mistaken for the Cygnus Solipsi Rai. Their face features are more bony and emaciated than the Solipsi Rai and they have bigger eyes. They wear black uniforms with silver patterns for high rankings. Their physical strength is also surprising despite of their size. Half insectoid by genetics, their way of communicating is mostly telepathic, accompanied by crackling sounds produced in their throat. They have four fingers, which is a recognisable feature. They have secret underground bases on Terra where they work in agreement with the US-military. They have usually large discoidal ships, with a completely neat and smooth surface.

CYGNUS
SOLIPSI RAI

Solipsi Rai

Unlike most races of small Grays, their society is not structured on a hive-matriarchy. They nourish interest in the development of other species. Some of them made alliance with the Ciakahrr Empire, the Orion Nebu and the Terran US government, working on technology in exchange for human materiel. They are involved in Dulce Base. This faction of Solipsi Rai is very active in the abductions, at service to the Maytrei, Kiily-Tokurit and Reptiloids. They also have been cloned and engineered with more efficiency, in order to produce more of them as slave workers, and we classify them as synthetic life-forms. Their ships are discoidal.

VELA
KIILY-TOKURT

Here are the Kiily-Tokurt tall-whites and the tall-gray Maytre as they are described by Stephen Chua, and depicted in my first book:

Origin: star "Suhail" in constellation Vela.They are 6ft tall, living up to 200 years, and also one of the oldest races in this galaxy. They are not members of the GFW. Very good shapeshifters but the one thing that gives them away is their dark eyes. Their true appearance is tall grey-humanoid, but they have reptiloid genetics. Very pale greyish skin, nearly white. Regularly mistaken for the Maytrei, who are not shapeshifters, have darker grey skin, uglier face and wider skulls. Kiily-Tokurit have two genders and are oviparous.

Kiily-Tokurt don't do hybridation programs but abduct for sexual slave trade and food market. Some work also as mercenaries. They are not allies of the Zetai, Ciakahrr, Maytra neither the Reptilian Alliance; they work solo and although they possess great weaponry power, they do not search for conflict. Frequent incidents with GFW forces are constantly occurring, regarding to their illegal business on Terra. Their ships are elongated black triangle with tree corner lights underneath plus a larger central one, and very recognisable. Compared to the USAF TR3B's, the KT ships do not make any noise, have sharp edges, are bigger, and possess a cloaking system based on quantum reflection (reflecting underneath what is above).

Male Kiily-Tokurt (right) represented with a female Kiily-Tokurt shape-shifted into a humanoid, to show the eyes stay black.

Andromeda Galaxy ("MEGOPEI")
MAYTRA

Maytra *(pl. Matrei)*, or Maitre, originate from two home planets in the nearest galaxy of Andromeda, that they name Megopei. They are your worst enemy, and the worst enemy of all races in this galaxy. Basically, they are considered as parasites by everyone except by those who managed to create alliances of mutual interests with them, that is to say: The Ciakahrr Empire and the Orion collectives. Of the same average height as humans, this race of hermaphrodites with long shaped face, elongated skull and long slim neck, carries indeed a very mean looking.

Their motivation is rage, hate and assimilation. Their ships are large, dark and discoidal with a circular row of lights plus a a large aperture underneath, and their insignia is a black inverted triangle on 3 lines and a red background.They have been visiting your planet since before the two last glaciations and tried to colonize it at many occasions, but were always interfered by either the Ciakahrr, the Anunnaki, the Council of Five or the Galactic Federation of Worlds. Not stopping there, they colonized 26 other planets. Abductions of humans are carried out openly by them, either for their own interest (slave traffic to mines on Terra's moon and Mars, as well as slave trade with other species, primarily the Reptilians), or in coalition with the US-Telos Alliance. The Maytrei have been involved in several tragedies throughout human history. Some of the worst plagues were inflicted by them with the knowledge and agreement of the Reptilians, who want the human population to never go over 8 billion.

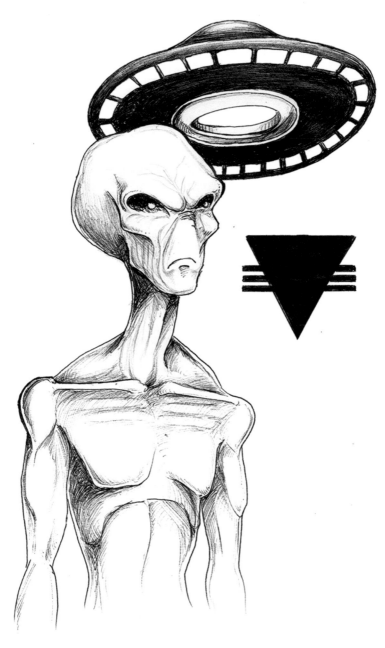

Maytre

AREA 51 RESIDENTS

Dow　　　　*Zeta Reticuli*　　　　*Solipsi Rai*

Kiily-Tokurt　　　　*Maytre*

The final combat

Elena:

Well Stevie you are very brave to tell us all of this. Do you feel safe now?

Stephen:

Ehm yes, I can be, because I've been looking over my shoulder for decades. You know, this is as far as... do I need any more, no! *(laughs)* I don't want anymore of this "BS". I mean what have I done to to hurt them... I haven't.

Elena:

No, and it is the time you know, when everyone speaks now, and all these Grays that are there, do you think as well... I think that the their existence on Earth is nearly touching an end, would you say that too?

Stephen:

I can feel that. At last, somebody is being able to chase them, take the rod and chase them off to the little corners, or wherever they're hiding. It's about time, because I'm really sick to death of these people, these beings, they've harassed me for so long... and if I can be part of doing the same thing as well, I'd be very glad to contribute.

Elena:

Yes, yes... but you can contribute as well, well hopefully you will be heard. If somebody thinks you'll be needed somewhere, and you can contribute as well scientifically, with everything you've learned and understood, so I think it's only good ahead, for everyone. And because I know you told me there's this Maytre entity that is sent like a dog to torture you, because they don't want you to remember, but you've overcome this creature, you have managed to get rid of it and take over, as incredible as it can seem. We are more powerful than them, we just need to know it.

Stephen:

But even then it was a very, very painful experience, emotionally and physically. It's like I mean they have unusual powers as well, like trying to rip the soul out of my body, you see blood coming out of my torso, where the shoulder would be. I was being attacked first by a tall thin shadow being. It came up from behind me at home. I could sense it and lashed out with a kick. I could feel hard contact with it and terrible burning pain on my heel. However, that being was sent flying into the wall where it left a dark imprint with a hard impact. Over the next several months I was being observed by people in black helicopters.

A few weeks later, I woke up one night with some energy dragging me from my chest and torso. I could see and feel my soul being drawn out. I resisted regardless of pain and shock. I could see a portal and on the other side were 3 Maytre. They wore a bluish type of cloak and gown with that typical triangle symbol with 3 stripes. They were working some kind of energy spell on me. It felt like a losing battle until I saw a massive wave of swirling energy blast through that portal, from behind me, sending the 3 tumbling and the portal was shut. I then collapsed.

I awoke with a very large being removing some probes from my chest and head. I could hear him telling me that he is just making sure the damage to my heart was corrected. *"Your soul is strong",* he told me. It was then that I could see the being. He had no hands like ours but long elegant fingers, that were so gentle. I somehow knew he was a Mantid, known to be excellent doctors. We actually chatted. He wanted to make sure I wasn't brain damaged. I called him "Dr. Trixy" (his language had a lot of clicks and the human tongue cannot pronounce the words) and he was pleased. I fell asleep. I do know that I'm one that never gives up. You won't get it out of me *(laughs).*

Elena:

They're going to go anyway soon, so it's good now. Well thank you so much for all these informations, all your memories from the Area 51 and before I ask you more cheerful questions, is there anything else you remember you wanted to share?

Stephen:

I'm sure more memories will come back, more fine details. Oh yeah, very important! The Maytre feeds of your energy as well. They torture me because the emotions of negativity, when it's very extreme, they absorb that energy from me and they get very, very strong because of that. In the presence of deep love, they fall apart.

Elena:

This is crucial...

Stephen:

You can literally make them fall apart, remember that, people, they cannot hold on to you, they cannot hold on to high energy, they just cannot. It's like... it's a fire on a flower, it shrinks instantly. You know, you destroy them instantly. It's very important.

Elena:

So, rising your vibration.

Stephen:

Yes, vibrations of love from somebody else too, they back off from it. They cannot touch it, they're so afraid of that energy, in fact, that... I heard it scream, one time. I heard this Maytre just scream, one time.

Elena:

So, the energy of love, and laughter?

Stephen:

Yes, yes! Develop that! Every morning start and every evening before you sleep...

Elena:

Have a good laugh.
(laughters)

Stephen:

I'm laughing a lot more these days.

Elena:

And the more you laugh, the more he's going away, your shadow "not friend".

Stephen:

Yeah the evil bunny.

Elena:

When good beings work hard to tell us: rise your vibration, rise your frequency, by feeling centered, peaceful and happy, and laughing, and love, that's not nonsense, it's really true!

Stephen:

It's real truth.

Elena:

You've experienced it yourself.

Stephen:

As part of my training in the martial arts, in the early 80's, I was asked to lead meditation sessions with Tibetan temples, you know, imagine having 200 monks and then they're following you *(laughs)* ! Anyway, I don't use those Alpha waves, I bring them up to Gamma waves, very different. Why I use Gamma waves: when you focus on Gamma, you can't help but being focused on joy. You want the joy, you want the sovereignty, the independence, your personal power, and you feel good and not sad after, after it all. So focus on the happiness. If you can develop the Gamma waves in the brain, it's so much the better!

Elena:

So the feelings of happiness, joy, inner joy and simple laughter, create Gamma waves?

Stephen:

Yes, you expand Gamma waves in the brain. We all have Gamma waves but very small amounts, usually. Too much meditation is done on Alpha, why that is not so great, because you're expecting somebody to tell you what to do. You want to tell the energies what you want, not the other way around.

Elena:

So Gamma waves are something that you can produce by this sensation of joy and happiness, and this rises your vibration, and creates Gamma waves that just radiate from you, that's what you say?

Stephen:

And also because of that you also raise your creativity. So much greater than Alpha waves.

Elena:

So you naturally create the Gamma waves when you create this feeling of joy and happiness. and the most entities like the Maytre or the dark entities, they can't approach it burns them?

Stephen:

Yeah the energy is too strong.

Elena:

That's why they try to scare people, too...

Stephen:

Yeah, and your Gamma disappears.

Elena:

And then you create something else that they feed of.

Stephen:

Yeah. I mean you want to be reaching up to the fifth dimension and not falling back into the lower third.

Elena:

So if everyone was trying to do this...

Stephen:

The Earth would be very different, yes. You find the plants will grow better too. Maybe if you have a garden, you keep doing that and you have better flowers, better vegetables, better fruits...

Elena:

Any other advice to create these Gamma waves, radiate them?

Stephen:

Meditation, first thing in the morning, or like what you did for me was to send me those tuning forks, you use the gamma ones and your brain will pick up on it very fast, or alternatively if you have a Tibetan bowl, a singing ball, most of them are tuned to G. So pick one up and use it.

Elena:

Wonderful... Any kind of special Hertz frequency or it's just G?

Stephen:

No, G. See, the real Tibetan bowl it has like seven types of metal. Gold is one of them, silver is one them, platinum as well, so a real original one can be pretty pricey but you don't have to go to all the way there. Let's get one that's tuned to G.

Elena:

And this creates higher frequency.

Stephen:

Yes, because of where it is when you do that, you feel your your energy centers, your chakras are resonating with the bowl, when you do it. And if you're very adventurous, get a huge one, like what I did one time. Initially when I used it, there was almost no sound *(Laughs)* because I didn't have enough energy. I learned to provide energy and it starts to ring like a bell, and everybody was staring at me. It was making so much noise, it was so loud. Nobody's ever made this thing ring so loud before. It is very energy sensitive.

Elena:

That is impressive. How do you see the future of humanity?

Stephen:

Full of promise. It is full of promise because from the time when I grew up and now... the time when I grew up it was everybody fighting for scraps, and then those few people living like kings. But more and more I see the controls starting to fall apart. You know being a banker I can tell that the banking system won't change and I would see that a new kind of cryptocurrency would work. But somebody must go and destroy the old first, meaning, to be fair, you have to get rid of the unfairness. Crooked money. Get rid of it. And then this new cryptocurrency can be unbreakable.

Elena:

What about the free energy?

Stephen:

What the free energy only requires is one large company making use of a new technology, and the floodgates will open. What I'd like to see is engines being replaced, engines and motor cars being replaced, because there will be immediate adoption by people, everybody will want it. And we can start, very quickly.

Elena:

Do you think what we've learned about alien technology of course will be integrated in our new devices?

Stephen:

It must, because they're so far ahead. At the very least, use their principles. You see, the development of technology is really a spiritual thing. If highly spiritual you are, well you can control the AI, not let AI control you.

Elena:

The power of the spirit. It is a new age where you are in a way a precursor. You are a representative of humans of the near future, because of your developed natural abilities. Do you think that humans will be like you? You are a step ahead because your abilities activated.

Stephen:

Well once it's shown, all you need is one person just to get started. A lot of other people will follow.

Elena:

Where we go one, we go all, as they say. What it takes is just that somebody starts it. Do you see Humans working hand in hand with benevolent extraterrestrials? Not those you've had misadventures with but other ones. Have you felt them near?

Stephen:

Yes, I believe that it was gonna happen. You see, people remember the nasty things more than they remember the pleasant ones. Sometimes, beings that you come across in your life might be an ET and you don't even realize that. They gave you a little bit of advice, they give you a bit of hand, as they say "the angels among us". I mean I've had people, so-called people, giving me advice, pointing me in a certain direction, and I have no idea who they are! And just a little bit later on, looking for them, I couldn't know where they are! They suddenly vanished.

Elena:

I think you were well looked after. Well I mean if you're still alive, and victorious now, after all you've been through...

Stephen:

Even that horrible car accident, in trying to get rid of the Maytra, actually. I came up without a scratch, which was quite astounding because you know, all the medical emergency services people came around, expecting the worst, and yeah nothing happened to me *(laughs)* not one scratch! Even my my friend who was driving the car, not one scratch on her. So I mean, how come?

Elena:

You have good protection and probably benevolent Ets. Why not people linked to who you are, your family, who knows. I was thinking more of a galactic family or...

Stephen:

Oh I really wish to know them.

Elena:

I'm sure they take care of you.

Elena:

Thank you so much, it's been two hours we have been talking so you must be very tired. Maybe we will speak again another time, I wouldn't like you to get too tired, and to mind yourself. So I don't know how to express my gratitude on behalf of all those who are listening, for your bravery, your resilience, your strength and your courage to speak now. And on behalf of everyone, we honor you and we thank you, and we are very privileged to get to hear what you had to say, Thank you so much, and is there anything, a message you would wish to pass on to humanity in these times?

Stephen:

Thank you for your kind words. For humanity: don't lose Hope! If you don't see Hope anymore, so look to who and what you want to be, how far do you want to go. It's now a message of Hope: "be". Thank you.

Elena:

Thank you very much. Gratitude.

Stephen:

Namaste /|\

• • •

Email, March 3 2020/ Elena Danaan to Stephen Chua

Hi Stephen
How are you today?

Email, March 3 2020/ Stephen Chua to Elena Danaan

overslept. but not well.
blackouts.
thanks for putting up the youtube
difficult to spell words

Stephen Chua

Email, March 4 2020/ Stephen Chua to Elena Danaan

Dear Elena
how did the youtube turn out?
I wasn't able to listen...too ill

Stephen Chua

Email, March 4 2020/ Elena Danaan to Stephen Chua

8000 views, and so many amazing comments. It has been shared a lot......
I was holding the protections up the whole time, being with you to protect you.

Email, March 4 2020/ Stephen Chua to Elena Danaan

You have such a loving community. Wonderful comments.
Thank you all.

Stephen Chua

Email, March 7 2020/ Rebecca Cheng to Elena Danaan

Hello Elena:

I am Rebecca Cheng, Stephen's friend.

I am accessing stephen's mail to contact you.

Stephen passed away Saturday.

Thank you.

Rebecca

• • •

When I received this email from Rebecca Cheng, Stephen Chua's partner, I broke down in tears with deep sorrow. The shock, the guilt I felt for having helped him getting his revelations out into the public arena, and the tragedy of the conditions of his death... it was so tough. "They" wanted to shut him down for a long time, and after he managed to get his truth out, more memories were rushing back.

Stephen could have told so much more information about his stay at Area 51, I knew well that his revelations were only the top of the iceberg. "They" killed him before he could say more. Nonetheless, the few he revealed was enough to rock the world of Disclosure.

• • •

CHAPEL RIDGE FUNERAL HOME - STEPHEN YANG LIANG CHUA
Singapore October 19, 1960 ~ Markham Canada March 6, 2021
Obituary

Stephen, Yang Liang Chua comes across as a being of multiple roles. The roles he displayed, is as in the eye of the beholder. Stephen would be that being, who understood and help achieve other's desires, need, or want. Allowance, acceptance, and focused attention to listen with openness of mind, heart, and soul, providing individual a safe place and peaceful.

He was born in Singapore, but his extensive adventures, life experiences were not confined to Singapore as he travelled extensively to various countries on business, work, and pleasure. He shared his knowledge, wisdom, expertise wherever he was. When he was in the military, he believed and practiced that not a single person be left behind. He was a true leader, he practiced what he preached. He was an inspiration to his fellow solders. Besides being in the battlefield, he was flying to various countries providing humanitarian assistance, especially those areas where the government officials were corrupt and in other cases, surrounded by bandits.

I have witnessed his "Leadership, Guide, Mentorship". He loved banking and finance. He negotiated with business individuals successfully, for both parties with the "win, win" outcome. He mentored the youth entrepreneurs at the YMCA Business Centre in Markham for many years. His leadership, mentorship, guidance and writing contribution to the COFN (Canada One Family Network) in Markham was a stupendous highlight. He was a natural born writer; ghost writing skill was amazing. It extends beyond to writing lyrics, he plays guitar beautifully and sing as well. When he passed away, he was writing his life story. Perseverance was what allowed him to overcome every day's health challenges, but he continued with a "smile".

He made others lighthearted and happy with his humours and funny jokes. One of his friends from Connecting Conscious mentioned, how she hears his laughter, and remember his incredible resilience for life. Stephen's connection with Mother Earth is reverence and compassion, he found solace and bliss. For guidance and protection, it was his maternal grandma, whom he adored, loved, revered, and trusted. He touched so many lives all around the world, he will be greatly missed! I will always treasure his friendship, he remains my best friend, who showed me compassion and love. Loving Kindness.

Rebecca Cheng

AFTERMATH

As detailed at the start of this book, Stephen Chua connected me to Dr. Michael Salla and the rest is history. A few weeks after the video of my interview with Stephen was out on YouTube, I received a comment underneath it, of someone named "Jeff Koh". It was for the most intriguing and even though I replied to him asking for more information or at least contact details, he never followed up. Here was his message:

"I'm Singaporean, Stephen has done us proud. I am honored to have been under his command for a brief period of time under 1st commando. Thank you for this disclosure. It is of highly valuable information for the whole humanity. Dracos had be stopped and together with the Cabals , they must be removed and prevented from pulling the string behind the scenes! Its sad I don't see any fellow Singaporean here in the comments. Shows how misinformed, state controlled and the tight surveiliance we are in..."

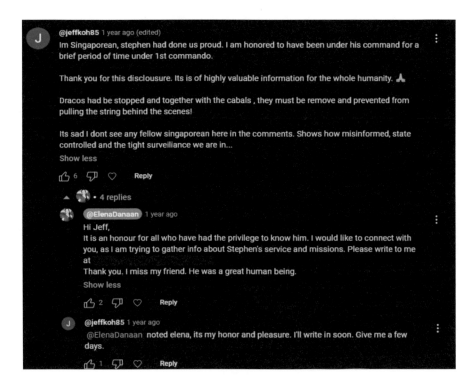

Supersoldiers & Extraterrestrial Agreements:

Interview with Elena Danaan on Death of Stephen Chua

Courtesy Dr. Michael E. Salla Ph.D.

What follows is a transcript of the interview published on March 12, 2021, on YouTube (https://youtu.be/7Qo-lgpLaHw). The transcript has been edited to remove redundancies and grammatical errors.

Acronyms: ED – Elena Danaan; MS - Michael Salla

MS – Well, welcome everybody. Aloha this is Dr Michael Salla and I'm very pleased to be with Elena Danaan who has some really interesting information to share with us about an interview she did with a super soldier who was active in the 1970s and 80s in Singapore and Malaysia. Her interview with him covered a lot of territory. So I just want to welcome you Elena to Exopolitics Today.

ED - Thank you Michael, I'm very honored to be on your show. Thank you.

MS – Yes, well this interview [with Stephen Chua] really got my attention because of his testimony but then he passed away in very unusual circumstances and there is a notice on your website where you posted "In memory of Stephen Chua" where you gave his full details and [notice of] him passing away. So why don't you just share with us what happened with Stephen?

ED – Well, [how[I met Stephen. I was approached by a spiritual group in Canada, Collective Consciousness, and [we] just [met] for spiritual things and he was part of it. I suddenly felt a lot of suffering coming from this person and I asked to contact him personally to offer him some healing and psychic readings and stuff like that.

He was delighted and we start to [have a] conversation and exchanges by email. He said to me that he worked in Area 51. I went, "oh my!" All I could see [was] all this is trauma and we started this conversation, this exchange by email. He started telling me things about it and I said, "wait for a minute, I wrote a book because I'm an experiencer and I got information from my extraterrestrial contact and it absolutely matches everything that you say!" Then I asked him a question. I said, "in my experience, I was told about a person called Dr Jenkins to contact in Area 51.

At the time I was 16 years old. I was totally frightened and I didn't do anything about it. [I asked] "Would you know about this person?" He got back to me and he said, "yes, of course, I met a Dr. Jenkins, a Professor Jenkins and he was in Area 51, and he was sent by the Vatican." I said "okay", and we didn't have an exchange for a while. Maybe a month or two and suddenly he sent me an email two weeks ago and said, "I'm ready to speak, please, if you want to interview me, I'll let you deal with all the Youtube stuff, I need to speak now. let's do it!" I said, "alright, because I have a Youtube channel I said "let's do it, okay. Are you sure, are you feeling safe for that?" He said, "oh, you know, I've looked over my shoulder all my life and I really want to do it please." So I said, "okay". We recorded this interview, but before we recorded it he said he was attacked energetically. He had blackouts and he suddenly wasn't feeling safe and he was speaking about Maytre extraterrestrials which are Tall Grays. I said, "last chance to withdraw Stephen if you want. Are you okay?" He said, "please, let's do it as soon as possible!"

So, we recorded this interview. He told me everything about his life, his experience in Area 51, his experience in Malaysia fighting Reptile beings in caves and everything....

After the interview, it was a Friday night, I said, "okay, let me edit it to hide your picture and do it anonymously and put some editing on it." He said, "okay, but be quick". On the Tuesday ... he sent me another email. He said, "will you please hurry up and put it up!" So, I say 'okay are you sure?" [He said] "Yes!" I put it up and on the Tuesday night in the middle of the night. I aired it on Youtube and on the Saturday I received an email from his family saying that he [had] passed away.

MS – Okay, so just to be clear here. You did an interview with him on February 26 [2021] which was a Friday and he urged you to publish the interview on your Youtube channel as quickly as possible, because he was starting to experience some symptoms of some kind of sickness, and and so you add the interview on March 2nd live streamed it and then on March 3rd, essentially the day after your interview with him went live you got the email from his family saying that he was dead.

ED - On the Saturday.

MS - On a Saturday, well I mean that obviously is very suspicious, the timing and the fact that he was in such a hurry for you to publish the interview. Do you think he was aware that the contents of his interview was something that was putting his life at risk?

ED - Yes, and I gave him many times the chance to withdraw, not to do it but he was so determined, you know. So I said okay.

MS – So, it was really, you know, you were concerned, you felt that there was something dangerous here for him and you gave him the opportunity [not to release the interview] but he felt that this was important. That [interview was] almost like his last contribution....

He was really seeing that this was something he wanted to offer humanity, the information that he had to share and he was willing to take the risk, and he paid the price for that.

ED - Yes and it is horrible for me as well because ... I gave him the choice many times and he was very determined. You know because he trusted me, because we were starting to be friends and I was an experiencer, I had contacts as well. So he knew I believed him and it just happened like this because I was there at that moment that that was all, you know, I was there at the right moment, and I was a person he trusted in that very moment, you know, and so that's how it happened, and oh my god.

MS – So, he was someone that had really important experiences as a super soldier, shared those experiences with you, encouraged you to publish those experiences knowing full well that his life was at risk, and only a short time after the interview was aired he was dead in suspicious circumstances. He had essentially intimated to you that this this was a possibility that he could be killed for sharing this.

ED - He didn't say that, but he was I suppose feeling threatened, because I told him, "are you feeling safe?" And I said it even during the interview, "are you really feeling safe?" He says "oh, like, whatever, you know, I've been looking over my shoulder all my life, you know!" And he looks so calm in this interview, like [the] release of a burden. It just released it out of him. It was like it took it out of him because he was really damaged, you know, they really damaged him. And you know, I said in a few words I wrote on my channel, Stephen was a sniper and I said, "may his last shot be his best!" May he be the whistleblower that just collapsed the building [dam], you know, because he must be honored for his courage, honestly.

138

MS -So you are in touch with his family and maybe his family would be able to share more information. Is that something you're willing to do? You know, I mean, because he says that he worked with the Singapore military for 10 years which is when he had these experiences and that he reached the rank of colonel at a very young age [21] because of his special abilities. So he was certainly someone quite exceptional…. I don't know if there's documentation or anything that his family is willing to share with you. I mean that would help because I think his case and the information he had to share is very important, it definitely dovetails with a lot of what I've been researching recently and I know what you've also covered in your book [*A Gift from the Stars*].

ED – Yes, absolutely, well he confirms things that are in my book which is a plus you know but indeed I've been contacted by his family. I don't want to expose them, but I am awaiting at the moment further information. I think they are still in [the process of an] autopsy, they haven't yet come up with a verdict. I am waiting for answers and I've asked for information regarding his military service here and there, whatever they could provide you know. So I'm waiting for this information and that's all I can say for the moment.

MS - Yes that's great, so I encourage listeners, viewers to watch the interview that Elena did with Stephen. It's online … but now I thought maybe it'd be good if we just cover some of the … [key] points in the interview you did with Stephen that was so important that he felt compelled to share this with you and get it out [to the public] and that [he] kind of experienced that unburdening that that you described. Well, he said that he was recruited into the Singaporean military at 18 general conscription that is mandatory there, and then eventually he was approached by officers associated with the Prime Minister's office in Singapore because of his very high IQ test scores. So, what happened when he got recruited by the office of the Prime Minister of Singapore what sort of things do you remember him saying happened?

ED – Well, first he was confronted to [join] because he had, I would say, psychic abilities. But I would say he was very intelligent and he was very sharp, very intelligent as a soldier, and they sent him on the most tricky missions. So he told me about two, three missions where he was involved in military operations where he was confronted with Reptilian beings, human hybrid Reptilians, they are totally Reptilians, and he used the words, the names—Ciakar is the word I have been given and I discovered as well that Alex Collier just used the same name too. It's so real, it's so confirming everyone. So he was involved in protecting … the Pakistan Prime Minister at the time who visited Malaysia [Singapore]...

MS – Benazir Bhutto.

ED - Benazir Bhutto, yes. So, he was involved in protecting her because the Prime Minister in Malaysia had received a message from the CIA that there could be an attempt of assassination of this Prime Minister Benazir Bhutto. So he was involved in closely bodyguarding her, this person. And well something happened that three people tried to kill her … and they [Stephen and bodyguards] ran after them. They killed two of them and the third one, Stephen approached this one. They caught him and he approached this assassin, and he could see scaly skin and that he looked human from afar, but from up close he had Reptilian skin and he was very shocked. And so this being was caught and taken away and he didn't know where they took him away. That was the first contact with the Reptilian being.

Then he was also called to an operation, I think ... he said it was in China I don't remember where there was one of these Reptilian beings terrorizing the populations.

MS – Japan.

ED – Japan, thank you. There's so many things in this interview and I'm still in shock. He got to catch this being and this being escaped in a flying saucer that landed, metallic gray flying saucer, he said. He went in and the saucer took off so that was very shocking.
MS - These were Ciakahrrs in that flying saucer or were these just the reptilian human hybrids?

ED - I think it was ... Ciakahrr. It was a Reptilian being anyway ... no sorry, I really apologize, it was a hybrid because he said that this one didn't have a tail because the hybrids don't have tails and the Ciakahrrs have a tail, the original ones, he said that. So, it was a hybrid. Third thing, a lot of children were disappearing in East Malaysia and he was sent to investigate with his team.....

MS - Can I just interrupt you there Elena, just to clarify something because I remember him saying something about working for the office of the Singapore Prime Minister.... What might be confusing is why is he doing missions in Malaysia? Was there a relationship between the Singapore Prime Minister and the Malaysian Prime Minister? Did their militaries cooperate because this was in the in the 1970s and Singapore and Malaysia had separated ... Singapore had seceded from Malaysia?

ED - I don't know.

MS – Okay, but essentially can you confirm he was working with the officer the Prime Minister of Singapore or of Malaysia? Because I remember him saying Singapore.

ED – So, it must be, I think, it's Singapore to be really clear. I think it's Singapore. I can get this confirmed by his family because he speaks very fast … it's difficult sometimes to understand. So yeah, he … was sent in these caves and he said it's big, huge caves where a plane can fly in and they came face to face with what he called a Ciakar Reptilian—a full Reptilian being. He said he was terrified because even though he was brave, he said that it's terrifying to see one. He describes it with the face, with the teeth and everything….

He said they have a claw here [pointing to her wrist], another claw here [pointing a few inches below the wrist] for combat. He said he had a gun and a beam energy gun…. This [Reptilian] being was pulverizing rocks, so they had difficulty to hide anywhere because he was shooting at them and the rocks would explode…. Stephen was a sniper and he had a special device with nuclear [device], a nuclear gun you know with protons. I absolutely [am] not knowledgeable in these things so I just repeat what he said. Maybe it makes more sense for other people and this nuclear weapon just collapsed the cave and the side of the mountain and that was the end of it. So that's what he said.

MS – Okay, so this was the incident with I think he said there were three, a group of three Ciakars that that were fully body armed and that the children were missing.

ED - Yes

MS - So the Ciakars were essentially … kidnapping children and using them for whatever they do there in these huge caverns. So there was a kind of fire fight that he and his team had with these Ciakars.

ED - Yes

MS - And when they came back the later, it was the next day in a helicopter, an especially quick helicopter, the cavern and the mountain where it was all under, had been collapsed. So the Ciakars had destroyed that facility and covered [it] up. So, it kind of confirms what a lot of people have been saying that Ciakars come to certain areas and they start becoming active whether it's kidnapping people, fighting soldiers, and then they leave.

ED - Yes and that totally matches with all legends in Asia, and this area in Asia especially in Nepal and Tibet where the people have legends about snake people, snake demons living in the caves and having confrontation with monks and you know stories like this. So that confirms local ancient legends.

MS – Well, I recently did an interview with a Brazilian author Fabio Santos who … had co-written a book with a Brazilian super soldier and he said that he was part of a planetary intervention force that was sent to fight with or monitor or engage or provide protective services for VIPs in situations involving extraterrestrials. And he described similar incidents to what Stephen encountered…. Stephen's experiences very much match this Brazilian super soldier's experiences in providing … protective services to VIPs in situations involving extraterrestrials … and that's what Stephen says he was doing, that he did it for the Prime Minister's office in providing protection for Benazir Bhutto that this is one of their jobs, you know, to provide protection and also to fight against some of the extraterrestrials that go into these areas.

ED – Yeah, this is amazing, yeah, absolutely, wow, that's exactly what he told me. He was asked to do this this job of protection and the CIA probably knew. You know, the CIA doesn't have a good name when we start to talk about these things.

MS – Well, you know many of the things that Stephen described in terms of his special skills, his training and then being sent off to do these special missions around the world with different governments, I mean he did it in Malaysia, he went to China, he went to Japan and so it seems that world leaders have a network of these super soldiers that are trained to engage or fight or interact with extraterrestrials and they draw upon this international network and this is what was happening with Stephen, which matches this Brazilian super soldier that Fabio Santos wrote the book with. So we have independent sources saying that there is this planetary intervention force of highly trained special forces soldiers who go and do the bidding of world leaders in situations involving extraterrestrial life and technology.

ED – Wow, yeah, I'm impressed, wow, yeah. And he said then, shortly after he was approached by a kind of committee he had difficulty to name it. They were coming from America and I said, "was it the CIA?" He said, "no something darker and more hidden." He didn't want to say it or he didn't know. He said he didn't know but I was sensing in him … [that] he didn't want to tell. He was too scared to tell it, so I didn't insist. So, an organization linked with the US came to approach him, and did four IQ tests to him, to recruit him. They told him all this because [they said] "you are so good, we want to send you to University in England." And he said, "okay, right I'll do this test." And he passed this IQ test and because it came out that Stephan had cognitive abilities, he could create a very powerful amount of gamma waves with his brain and that was interesting [to] these secret services.

So then shortly after the Prime Minister, for whom he was working, said to him, "oh I received an order from these people that they want to borrow you to work in Area 51." They wanted to have him like forever [permanently] but the Prime Minister of Singapore he wanted [Stephen].

Yeah it was Singapore ... he didn't want to let him go because he wanted to keep him. He said, "okay, I allow you only two weeks, [you] have him for two weeks." ...

[Note: There were actually two separate sets of tests that Stephen Chua underwent. The initial IQ tests were completed by Singaporean military which brought him to the attention of the Prime Minister, and then later, after the US secret organization had heard about Stephen's results, he was tested by them for gamma brain waves. Stephen was subsequently offered a position at Area 51.]

MS - We will get to his Area 51 experiences shortly but I really want to ... emphasize this point that even though Stephen was working with the office of the Prime Minister of Singapore, because this was dealing with extraterrestrial life that he would often be sent off to these different countries whether it was China, Japan, Malaysia to engage with extraterrestrials that are interacting amongst us.... This kind of matches the testimony of other super soldiers but I also want to point out that this also matches with what the Prime Minister of Russia, [Dmitry] Medvedev said in 2012 in a hot mike incident. He said that there was a force or an organization that monitored extraterrestrials living amongst humanity, and he said that this was an organization that ... the President of Russia would be briefed about when he came into power. He would receive two folders or two files. One dealing with the nuclear codes for their weapons and the other dealing with extraterrestrials amongst us.... And a worldwide organization monitoring extraterrestrials [existed]. So, we have here the former Russian President Medvedev confirming that there is this worldwide organization set up to monitor and interact with extraterrestrials living amongst us. And then we have these super soldier accounts, like with Stephen and with this Brazilian super soldier, as well, confirming that this planetary organization exists.

ED – Yes, absolutely and uh when he speaks about this secret organization that hired him maybe it is linked to it. I don't know it's just supposition.

MS – Okay, all right, so Stephen had these special skills, he's working with this world organization on behalf of the Singapore Prime Minister's office to do different things, and then at a certain point some Americans noticed that he has this unique ability in emitting gamma rays and that's somehow related to a pilot being able to interact with the technology of flying saucers or anti-gravity craft.
So, he goes to Area 51 and gets trained. Do you want to cover a little bit about what happened at Area 51, who Stephen met, and what his experiences were there?

ED – Yes, so as soon as he arrived there ... they told him that he would be hired and trained very quickly to pilot an F-15 plane, [an] F-15F plane, he said, and that it is a program aimed to pilot these planes by thought. So they were studying and developing this technology of piloting planes by thought, by the mind. The reason why, it's because it's a faster response and it's more reliable and faster in combat than having to rely on mechanical controls. So that was the purpose of it. So that was why he was hired there to experiment with him and develop this ability. Because as Stephen said, "so how was it happening?" They were injecting a serum in the pilots that this serum was super activating the brain functions but the problem is that all the pilots were dying after a while because it was mushing the brain like mash. And he was passing all the tests. He was strong and ... he didn't die from it, but you know it was a heavy thing to do. So, he speaks about how he was put in the plane and ... how this was all working. So that's what he was doing there. Then when he arrived he said, "there's a huge protection around Area 51, huge but once you're in it, you're kind of free to go wherever you want more or less because it's so protected from outside, so you're okay inside."

You can't get in, can't get out." So anyway as soon as he arrived he was with military guards and they were carrying super heavy weapons inside, and Stephen asked, he said, "just one question, why are you carrying these weapons inside, what for?" And one guy told him, "it's to protect you against the Grays!" "What Grays, he [Stephen] said? "Oh, the alien Grays … the Grey Alliance" [the guard replied]. And that's how it was just revealed there are ETs in there and there are Grays. So the Gray alliance is an alliance of Gray races that are very malevolent to humans on Earth, you know, they are from Orion…. During his time there he met three different ET races, which were not benevolent at all. They were working closely with the military there.

MS - So we need to first clarify that when we're talking about Area 51, we're talking about the S4 facility there because Area 51 has two facilities. One is at Groom Lake, which is where they built the spy planes for the Air Force and the Navy and that's a kind of cover program. But at Papoose Lake they have the S-4 facility where they have the flying saucers, the ETs and all of this really highly advanced anti-gravity developments going on. But what I thought was very interesting in the interview with Stephen was that he said that the Grays were not very good themselves at building technology that they really relied on humans to build the technology. The Grays were good at kind of like sharing the information on how to do it, but they weren't so good at building it. Can you just explain what was going on there.

ED - The first word he employed was lazy, but that tells a lot because Grays had a work force there. Humans who are very happy to know, to learn, how to build this ship, you know, so why would they do the job themselves? They were just employing workforce there…. What I understood of what Stephen was describing these beings. They were [displaying] very superior behavior.

Like we are superior and you humans are just, you know, slaves or like primitive beings. That was the attitude they had so it's totally understandable. They surely can build their own ship, but it's totally understandable that they were taking advantage of getting the humans there happy to build these things for them, you know. So that's what I understood.

MS - Yes so that's a very important point because it means that this alliance you know we're talking about the Gray [Orion] Alliance, the Ciakahrrs, the Reptilians, they have really advanced technologies, but they aren't good at building the technologies themselves. What they're good at is forcing other races, in particular humans, whether we're talking humans on Earth or human looking races elsewhere in the galaxy to build these technologies. They're kind of like conquerors. They kind of come in, they conquer a place they get the people there to build new technologies, which will help them move forward in their planetary conquests.

ED – Yes, indeed, and as Stephen could confirm the Tall Grays are using the small Grays as a slave workforce but the small Grays are mainly all clones. There are few original biological small Grays left. They're all cloned and synthetic life forms and things like that.

MS – Yeah, this kind of matches with one of the things that I got from interviewing Corey Goode who says that humans are building on Mars … advanced technologies that they trade with up to 900 different extraterrestrial races…. He says that was what he was told by a manager of a corporate facility on Mars that they were building technology and trading it with up to 900 different ET civilizations… What Stephen told you kind of corroborates that the ET's aren't great at building technologies themselves that they rely on subservient races like humans to build it for them.

ED – Yes, indeed Michael and Stephen at the end of in the interview just blew my mind when he started to speak about Mars, saying that one day he met technician people, he said not military, [but] technicians trained to build [things], coming out of a shuttle. This shuttle was coming back from Mars. And I went, "what?" The shuttle was coming back from Mars bringing back human Earthling technicians who told him that they were there to build facilities for ETs. So these technicians were describing the bad conditions of the flights that it was very rough.

Then that there [was a] Reptilian race [that] was their boss to build this facility they were coming from, but that there was … also Gray races. There were many people out there on Mars but basically Mars belongs to aliens and they use humans to build their facilities. And there are some kind of treaties that humans can have their own facility there but it's just under the direction of these ETs. He was saying something, this technician, to Stephen: "if you don't do how they [the aliens] ask you, they throw you outside and you die in two minutes." That's what they were saying.

MS - That's very important these agreements with extraterrestrials and human leaders. That's one of the things that really got my attention about claims that these agreements go back to around 600 A.D. where there were agreements reached between human leaders and extraterrestrials, where the extraterrestrials would no longer openly appear…. They wouldn't go into cities and be worshipped as gods, but now they would operate behind the scenes. Secretly just communicate with world leaders and they would go to different places where they would fight with soldiers or take people. These agreements go back over a thousand years. Do you know anything about these agreements going back that far?

ED - I have been told, yes, that there are agreements with Reptilian races now [from a] very long time ago. And there has been a second wave of agreements with the Gray alliance in 1954 and around it. That was made with the MJ-12. Eisenhower tried to stop it, he wasn't okay with that. So I have had that confirmed many times.

MS - Oh good, so that's important that these agreements with the Reptilians predate the agreements that were reached in 1954-55 with President Eisenhower and the Gray alliance. That the agreements with the Reptilians go back much further. Some people say up to around 600 A.D. um and that kind of would explain, you know, situations like what Stephen was describing. Where you would have these Reptilians operating in places like Japan and China and Malaysia, abducting children and having fights with soldiers and the world doesn't hear about it. It's all done secretly so it's confirming that these leaders keep it secret amongst themselves and when they have a situation that they contact this worldwide organization to get super soldier sent, to go into these areas and find and engage with the extraterrestrials or the Ciakahrrs.

ED – Yes, that totally matches with what Stephen says.

MS – Yeah, that is really incredible information. Unfortunately you were only able to interview Stephen once. Do you have any kind of sense like what else he had to share or what it is that may have led to him being targeted by this planetary organization?

ED - Well he was saying that they had tried to wipe his mind, his memory, before allowing him to leave Area 51. But Stephen had a very special mind abilities so he was able to remember a big part of it, but he was saying to me that he was working very hard to try to remember all the rest.

Because he was saying that he was suspecting that the Maytres, the Tall Grays, had done something to him and he couldn't put the finger on it, you know. He was fearing them really….. After the interview I sent him an email to say oh here is the recording of the raw Zoom meeting and i'm going to edit it ,and maybe in the future, if you have more things coming [back], we can do a second interview. And he replied, "we will see. I will think about that." So he wasn't sure but I knew that in the same time he was working hard to try to find his memory. So you know i'm sure he would have had other elements coming but I think they didn't want him to say more, you know. Probably I think he, yes, he felt the moment because the tone of the emails changed.

We were talking about spiritual things and healing and the power of the mind and things like that. And we were not talking about Area 51 anymore because I knew it was something that was too hard for him. I just allowed it to go but suddenly one day after two months, no news, [he writes] "I'm ready to speak. Let us do it as fast as possible, as quick as possible. I'm ready. I'll let you organize Youtube." Suddenly I don't know what happened. Suddenly he was probably feeling threatened in some way. He said he had blackouts when he sent me this last email on the Tuesday following the interview, four days just after the interview, saying … "please put this interview live however it's edited or not edited" He said, "because I have blackouts and nose bleedings." I said, "oh my gosh!" And I reply, "are you really sure?" And he said, "please, please!"

MS – Okay, so he was really intent on getting that information out.

ED – Yes.

MS - There seemed to be something happening that was very suspicious behind the scenes. So we do know that there is this international organization that has super soldiers trained to find and monitor and engage and have firefights with extraterrestrial entities all around the world. By revealing his secrets … it's very possible that this organization wanted to stop him from revealing more.

ED – Maybe, probably that … really makes sense so i don't know.

MS - Okay well, I just wanted to give you the opportunity to maybe share a little bit about where people can find out more about you and the work that you do in raising awareness of extraterrestrial life on planet Earth. So please just tell people where they can go.

ED - Thank you. I have a YouTube channel elenadanan where I put everything I know on it. So there are interviews, and there are contacts with extraterrestrial beings. But what I think really helps as well, it's a book I have written a *Gift from the Stars*…. It's only on Amazon at the moment but that's it. So, I tell in this book my personal experience of being abducted by Gray aliens and rescued by Nordics and so I tell everything about it and the knowledge I gained from it, what they told me. So, this is available on Amazon and that's how you can know about me.

MS - Thank you Elena. Well, I definitely would like to do a follow-up interview and talk about your book and some more experiences that you've had. You know, I'm particularly interested in what you have to share about Valiant Thor experiences but we'll cover that in another interview. So I want to thank you for coming and being a part of Exopolitics Today. Mahalo,

ED - Thank you very much Michael thank you.

**

Maybe other brave soldiers who knew Stephen Yang Liang Chua and worked with him will come forward, for times of disclosure are here. Stephen was an extraordinary human being. I don't know how he could survive all what he went through, but he did, to bring the truth when the right time had come. He was a hero and the courage it took for him to perform the final act is unfathomable. Stephen knew the consequences, and he faced them with honor. May his spirit and his legacy inspire many.

Elena Danaan, Ireland, April 2023.

Made in United States
Troutdale, OR
08/26/2023

12261507R00093